ACCELERATED LEARNING

Improve Your Memory and Reading Speed and Unlock Your Brain's

(Sharpen Your Focus So You Can Master Any Skill and Outsmart Anyone)

Roderick Maldonado

Published by Jordan Levy

Roderick Maldonado

All Rights Reserved

Accelerated Learning: Improve Your Memory and Reading Speed and Unlock Your Brain's (Sharpen Your Focus So You Can Master Any Skill and Outsmart Anyone)

ISBN 978-1-77485-313-9

Legal & Disclaimer

The information contained in this book is not designed to replace or take the place of any form of medicine or professional medical advice. The information in this book has been provided for educational and entertainment purposes only.

The information contained in this book has been compiled from sources deemed reliable, and it is accurate to the best of the Author's knowledge; however, the Author cannot guarantee its accuracy and validity and cannot be held liable for any errors or omissions. Changes are periodically made to this book. You must consult your doctor or get professional medical advice before using any of the suggested remedies, techniques, or information in this book.

Table of Contents

Introduction

If you're currently reading the book then it's likely that you're someone who is looking to commit yourself to enhancing your performance in your life, whether it is in school, at your job, or any other area. Being having this book in your hands means the first step to achieving your goals. This might be a extravagant claim to make, but you'll discover the reason for making this assertion. The strategies we examine in this book will certainly let you gain more details and spend less time on it.

These tools are not just going to bring you satisfaction, but you'll likely feel more secure when you step into the classroom, workplace, or going about your day. We hope that you're as eager to learn about learning like I am. The reason I wrote this book is that a lot of universities and high schools do not provide the abilities to be able to learn effectively and speedily.

Teachers also believe that their students will naturally acquire these abilities however this assumption is untrue.

A lot of students aren't given the tools that they require to succeed in school. This is a problem that plagues students throughout their lives. This is the reason this book is out. Even if it's a little sooner than it should but at the very least, you'll be able to be able to learn in a efficient manner. Being able to learn efficiently and effectively can improve your skills today and in the future your life. This is particularly important in the age of information, where technology is constantly evolving.

The ability to master your studies can determine the kind of job you're capable of pursuing and excel in. A typical person has more than seven different jobs once they have graduated from college. The majority of these jobs are in fields that are not related to. If you can find an occupation and maintain it throughout your existence, then you're one of the most fortunate people in the world. The majority of people will be constantly updating their knowledge and skills to stay ahead of the curve.

The learning process outside of the formal academic class is usually accomplished by way of informal exploration. It is learning through interactions, social situations that are fun and connecting with other people. However school learning styles may affect the way teachers instruct. The current methods of teaching employed in universities and high schools don't take into consideration the way that brains function.

A few experts have pointed out that classrooms are exactly the opposite environment that your brain naturally skilled to learn in. Learning in the classroom as it is today is only useful only for a small portion of students.

The formal learning process in a classroom environment has led many to wonder if they really can learn. According to one study 82% of kids who entered school at the age of 5 or 6 believed positively about their abilities to learn. The same kids when they reach the age of 16 tend to be more negative, with just 18% believing that they are able to learn. If you're someone who has ever wondered the way they learn, this book might make you reconsider your abilities to learn.

Humans are extremely smart learners. Brains can be described as supercomputers. The main obstacle in making use of our brains is the lack of a guide on how to utilize our brains. This book is likely to serve as your guide for improving your learning abilities.

This book has an informal tone to serve a reason. If you picked an uninteresting and dull book , such as a textbook then you won't find it engaging enough. Learning to learn is a subject that requires full concentration and participation If you want to increase your capacity to learn. Therefore, changing the tone is intended to make the book simpler to read. It is a book that you should thoroughly enjoy perhaps even in your home for the weekend to go through it.

I'm hoping that you'll enjoy yourself through this book and the abilities it will teach you. In order to ensure you don't have to deal with lots of boring content, I've kept it out of the book. There's nothing but valuable and actionable information contained within this book, which is the level of efficiency that I would like you to strive for. There is a lot going on beyond this book, and to be respectful of this, I've made this book as thorough as is possible.

One last note that I'd like to make before leaving. One of the fundamental principles of fast-paced learning is to test your capabilities as you develop them. There are chapters within the book that have different questions types. Each test or quiz is intended to test your knowledge of the text. Although it might be tempting to skip a section, you'll discover that the information is worth the time and effort. If you've absorbed all the information from that previous chapter, be sure to reward yourself for your success prior to moving onto the next section. The time has come to begin the journey. Have fun!

Chapter 1: What to Learn the Most Effectively?

"Knowing your opponent is a fight that is half won."

The following excerpts are from The Art of War by Sun Tzu, Chinese philosopher

If you are looking to accomplish things with the greatest effectiveness, the first step is understand the people that are involved. In the case of study the subject, it's you.

It's likely that since the beginning of your schooling you've heard about people declaring that they are visual learners or auditory learners and so on. Perhaps you've wondered what kind of student that you might be, and perhaps you've even completed a test to find out. This chapter will provide additional characteristics of the various types of learning, to help you decide the one that fits your needs best.

There are a few points to keep in mind but. The answer you get from a test may not be the sole correct answer even if it appears to be to be consistent. Most of the time there is a mix of different learning styles. Also, your style of learning is able to change and evolve to the subject you're studying and the general attitude you display at the moment. The goal of this chapter is to help open your eyes to possible methods of learning and identify which can be beneficial to you.

Whitman College in Washington, USA states that four major learning styles are available. They prefer to refer to these preferences in the form of VARK: V stands for visual Aural or auditory reading, R for writing, and K for the kinesthetic (or the movement of your body). There are a variety of sources that add additional styles, like practical, outdoor and so on. However, these four primary categories will suffice for this book.

Visual Learners

Visual cues such as shifts in color, the position of things, striking patterns, can help to jog the memory of those who learn visually. They learn best using symbols or hierarchies as well as other types of media that convey words. If you find you trying to recall things based on the place it was in your notes as well as the colour you wrote an important point in, you're likely to be a visual student.

How do they process the information?

They are able to remember information from instructors who make use of grand gestures or descriptive language.

* Slides, posters and photographs - but not photos or pictures. Visual people learn the best by looking at pictures when there are patterns or designs, patterns whitespace, as well as other formats that highlight certain details.

* Films

* Flowcharts, diagrams, and flowcharts

* Use highlights, underlines or bolding colors for categorizing subjects.

How do they keep information?

* Trying to recreate diagrams, images or figures within their minds

Reconstructing flowcharts and diagrams from scratch

* Replacing symbols, drawings or symbols for words

What do they do to remember what they've learned?

* Relay information from visuals into Word format

* Drawing

* Recalling images and using diagrams

Aural/Auditory

People with auditory processing difficulties learn best by listening to or speaking information. Most often, auditory learners enjoy discussion groups or review sessions, speaking or talking about things or by using telephone, radio or email. They generally prefer to talk first, before analyzing the information and think about it prior to speaking. People who can recall facts based on what a instructor or classmate has spoke about are more susceptible to being auditory learners similar to those who prefer to take a test prior to taking an actual test.

How do they process the information?

* Participating in classes, review sessions, and group discussions to enhance current knowledge

• Explaining concepts and ideas to others (or them)

* Using voice recorders

* Describe visuals to others.

What can they do to keep the information they have?

* Asking for others to evaluate their understanding of a subject

* Quizzing other students or being challenged

Reading notes in summary out loud

* Listening to recordings of previously recorded lectures or studying sessions

Subvocalizing: Talking with yourself about the information you'd like to recall without reading your notes or book.

What do they do to remember the lessons they've learned?

* Repetition of the sounds/voices in their head , and then recording them on paper

* Keeping quiet in zones to aid in recalling information

Do not whisper questions or answers while taking an exam.

Writing and Reading

The people who learn the most through writing and reading are those who have an awe-inspiring interest in words. There are numerous sources that suggest that they do best in classrooms that are traditional, since the majority of methods of learning are based on textbooks. The outputs can be found from PowerPoint presentations as well as manuals, essays assignments, reports, and written exams. If you love making lists to record the information you've learned, or remember information by finding the answer to an earlier assignment, that could be your preferred method of learning.

How do they process the information?

* Making/reading lecture transcriptions that include headings, lists, and descriptions

* Reading/answering handouts, textbooks, manuals, assignments

* Recording notes

* Making essays

What can they do to keep the information they have?

* Notes to be rewritten

* Reading often

* Turn diagrams, charts, etc. into words

What do they do to remember the information they've learned?

* Making and responding to mock exams, as well as essays

* Arranging words in their connections

Kinesthetic

In contrast to writing and reading learners Kinesthetic learners typically struggle to learn in a traditional classroom in which students are required to sit at their desks and listen to a lecture that lasts from several hours or more on the subject of their choice. Learners who are kinesthetic need to move and are drawn to exercises and practical application of theories. They are most effective when they are asked to do cases studies and to practice.

Learners who are able to utilize a lot of their senses. If they are able to grasp the sensation, feel or taste something, they will likely remember the information. For them, the most effective teacher is the one with experience. They have a preference to learn from their previous experience or from their experiences with other people.

How do they absorb the information?

* Maximizing the utilization to the fullest extent of their sensory abilities.

* Participation in field trips and exposure activities

* Practical problem solving

* Errors and trials

* Exhibits, labs and simulations

How do they keep information?

* Using many examples

* Conducting case studies

* Taking short, regular study breaks

* Using the computer/writing/drawing when studying to activate the sense to touch

* Keeping track of things when exercising

Playing quiz games (ex., Jeopardy) while studying in a group

What do they do to remember the information they've learned?

* Exams that you can answer with mock questions

* Remembering experiments, etc.

* Reminiscing about a memorable experience - - whether your own or another person's

Most likely you've said, "That's me!" or "Yeah I did this" across all these categories. It's not unusual. Few people prefer one particular type of item however the majority populace is classified as "multimodal.'

There are two kinds of multimodal:

*Type I They are adaptable and can easily change their style of learning to their current circumstance. For instance in the case of studying history, they employ the writing/reading style, however, when they're doing lab work, they employ their kinesthetic approach.

The Type II These individuals are more strict in their learning approach in that they're not satisfied until they've had an output or input to the topic in all their preferred ways. Learning for them is usually longer, and many see them as slow learners. However the amount of work they put into learning about a particular subject could make them more proficient at the subject than the Type I might be able to.

Take a moment to reflect on your habits of study. Do you have a tendency to change your learning style according to the topic you're researching (a Type I tendencies) or do you have a tendency to switch between various learning styles on one subject before you think that you're prepared (Type II)? Understanding this is crucial to organize the remainder of your time studying efficiently.

Type I's have to know prior to time the strategies for learning a subject requires and then go over the topic multiple times using the same strategy to gain a better understanding. Type II's on the contrary, have to determine which style will yield better results for certain subjects to be able to include different styles to review later on.

Chapter 2: The Selective Learning

In the last chapter, we described the three primary aspects of our program of learning that include priming the pump, feeding the machine and finally, locking it into. The three phases follow a pattern that may be familiar that is planning, execution and some sort of revision, review or refinement.

The focus in this section, "Selective Learning," covers the first two phases. I've previously mentioned how crucial selection is to our speedy learning process. It's one of the main factors what differentiates the accelerated learning method from other methods in which you may have to navigate through hoops and miss out on classes prior to completing the classes that are useful.

The main benefit of doing independent study is that you do not have to endure the whims of your professors. You decide and design your study plan. You don't have anyone to answer to other than you, so there's no reason to not give you precisely what you want. If you don't find something that is relevant to the things you're looking to learn You can eliminate it. This brings to mind one of our main guiding principles that we must adhere to: concentrate. It's crucial to not move around in a random manner. The next chapter will focus on how we'll begin by defining our goals and then consider ways to break them down into manageable micro-goals.

Setting Goals and Redefining Yours

Now is the time that it's worthwhile to revisit the goals we established in the first chapter. Check your primary Goal Inventory. If you weren't able to finish this task first time it, consider doing this now. This is going to be the most focused at this point with the two first items on the list. I'll list them here to make it easier:

1)What is your ultimate goal? What knowledge or skill do you want to master? Give it a detailed description.

2)Visualize you at the ideal stage of excellence. What can you expect to accomplish that you aren't able to accomplish today? Define this with precision.

Between these two things between the two items, you must be able to sketch out the best way to proceed. However, rough plans aren't sufficient. The self-study program we create must be exact. This is part of what's going to distinguish this learning experience from any other you've had. As we've stated, you have control over this experience. This is a good aspect. You have the ability to choose what you'll need to know and what you do not need to learn. There's no need for a teacher who will direct you in a direction that you may not be interested in. This is generally a great idea, but it places the responsibility upon you to manage your personal education. You are accountable to yourself as a teacher and you must be able to take this seriously. The two other elements from the Primary Goal Inventory got at this. Here are the results (in the form of a shortened version):

3)Write an affirmation and claim that you are responsible for the achievement of this goal.

4)One more affirmation , this one that says that you believe that you are capable of doing it.

You are the teacher and you have a responsibility. Don't let it disturb your peace. This is all about being calm, as calmness is an essential element of any learning experience that is effective. However, you should do yourself a favor by confirming the promise you made to manage your learning in a responsible manner. The major part of this promise can be described as focus and selection. When we say selection, we are referring to the decision of which items to include and what not to incorporate into your plan of instruction. By "focus," we refer to the ability to, if required, separate chunks of information from the entire to be dealt with separately at specific time periods.

To help you think about this, here are some big-picture ideas I'd offer. At the beginning of your research, conduct an informal survey of your project to establish the boundaries of what you've learned and what you must be aware of. Think about a general overview of the matter. I prefer to think of it being conceptually "zooming across" to escape the detail level and see the larger image. Imagine your object as an outline of a map.

It could remind you that learning maps that we talked about as a method for visually impaired learners. That's no accident. In fact, what I am proposing as a mental exercise for your own informal use could be made into a map of learning and will serve as a useful tool when you plan your activities.

Then, imagine this map. The important details to learn include the zoomed-in map on which you can see street names. The zoomed-out map shows the entire nation. You can see major highways and interstates that show how everything is interconnected. If you're interested in knowing more about how to maintain your vehicle The big picture map will show the various systems that are involved that include transmission, fuel brakes, steering and more. The zoomed-in version will inform you about how the mechanical components work in each of these systems.

The first step is to grasp the larger versions of the maps. If you're bringing some prior knowledge regarding the issue, you may be able to sketch it off of your head. If not, a quick glance through your table of contents of any good book about the subject could be an effective step. In any topic, you'll be able to discover some key points from which to build your overview of the topic and perhaps begin the process of selecting by including or excluding topics when necessary.

Let's suppose you were interested in learning about the past of ancient Rome. For a review of the first two items of the

Primary Goal Inventory, for #1, perhaps you wrote, "I want to understand the past of the ancient city of Rome," and for the second item, one where the question asked you to explain your level of knowledge and expertise, you wrote "I would like to be able discuss the subject in a conversation. If it comes up at a social gathering I'd like to be able understand the comments of others and be able to contribute." It's fine. You don't need to become one of the top experts. You're not attempting to research an article or trying to become a professor in the past, but you need to know the fundamentals.

With that in mind there's still plenty of an opportunity to focus. By doing a bit of study, a glance at over the contents table in the history of Rome or even a great Dictionary or even Wikipedia, you'll gain a general understanding of the background you're studying. Are you looking to learn more about the Roman Kingdom and the Roman Republic or the Roman Empire as well as all three? Are you interested in the decadent era or the fall and decline? Are you looking for cultural and artistic expression as well as military history and the bigger than life figures? Are you interested in all of them? This is your opportunity to establish limits. You can include or exclusion.

Another item to add to your workbook. This is what we'll call it Your RGI.

1)List your goal that you have refined. You can go through different stages of refinement using this. It is possible to begin by redefining your goal in the event that you completed an exercise called the Primary Goal Inventory. You can then begin asking yourself questions about the parameters. Where does the body information or the pool of knowledge that you're interested in begin and end? If you're looking to learn computer programming, what languages would you prefer to add or eliminate? If you're interested in the field of psychology are you looking to study the field of developmental psychology? Abnormal psychology?

Revise and refine your ideas. Interrogate your wording. Try to be specific. Do some investigation and then figure out the overall idea - the road map which outlines everything. determine where exactly your journey will lead you. Continue to work until you've crafted a sentence or two that clearly defines the course of your study.

2)List your primary idea. What's the primary idea of what you're trying to master? This can serve as a guideline, to remind you of the direction you're heading. Always do your research when important.

If you've got a journal and you're keeping a notebook, you can put the Refined Goal Inventory alongside your primary goal inventory. Don't toss out the first document, as it's filled with affirmations that can be helpful in times of need to increase your confidence or boost your enthusiasm. In the next chapter, we'll discuss zooming into the map - taking the large vision of goals and breaking the subject into bite-sized pieces. Mindful encoded bits of information and micro-goals allow us to move in smaller steps.

Chapter 3: Acquire the Abilities and Familiarity

When you've reached the perfect mental, emotional physical, and mental state to gain new information, you must do what you can to improve your skills and get familiar with the knowledge you want to master. In the beginning, you must to establish a broad understanding of what you intend to study. A lot of students don't realize the significance of looking at the information in the broad spectrum prior to beginning their studies, and end up exerting a lot more time and energy studying excessive--and possibly irrelevant--information.

A Comprehensive View

It can be as difficult as solving a 1000-piece puzzle without a picture to base it off of. Although it's not difficult, it is more difficult to finish the puzzle if you don't know what the final result is expected to appear like. Naturally, it'll require a lot more time and will require a lot of guessing and figuring out work to accomplish. The same principle applies to learning new information or learning an entirely new skill. In the absence of a general concept of what the product is going to look like it will take an inordinate amount of hours and effort on irrelevant tasks trying to determine it. A clear understanding of what the result of your efforts will be will provide your brain with an idea of what you want to achieve and identify specific areas of work to do to achieve the desired result.

The process of learning by writing out your task from beginning to end can improve the efficiency of the learning process. It in turn, make it simpler to retain details later without having to constantly look back and skim through it all. Making a outline of your project isn't as difficult as it appears, and simply involves you looking through and skimming over all of the data you'll be learning and studying. An example of this is when you're about to begin an entirely new course. The syllabus will likely be provided along with a short introduction to the topic as well as a lesson plans on the first day of class, along with all the other learning tools you'll have access (such books, specific course online education platforms, Internet sources, etc.). Start by reviewing each of them and attempt to link your experience to the material that you'll learn. Think about the reason you're taking this course at all and then ask yourself what you'd like to accomplish at the end of the course done. This will give your brain a the motivation to work hard.

One of the most effective methods to gain a broad view of your studies is to go through and have an overview of the subject prior to the beginning of your course and each class afterward. It is recommended to make time for ten or fifteen minutes prior to classes to go over the subject to be covered the following day. It is sometimes difficult according to your schedule therefore, flexibility is essential. It could be as easy as a quick glance through chapters of a textbook which includes the content for the next day's lesson plans as listed in your syllabus. It's also extremely helpful to make use of one of the many free online sources. Today, nearly all teachers publish their materials, handouts, lesson plans, and studies guides on the internet for their class. Apart from this you can find a myriad of free open resources that available online to access any type of information you could ever want. You can view videos that you can watch on YouTube and MIT Open Courseware. However, it is important be cautious when accessing information that is public on the Internet that was not posted by your instructor, since the websites and videos can be uploaded by anyone and frequently contain inaccurate information, while making a convincing sound. Similar is the case for online Encyclopedias such as Wikipedia and Wikipedia, which is why it's vital to ensure that your sources originate from reliable sources.

The same strategies when you are the task of reading to a class. Before you read the entire section you could skim through them to get a sense of what you're likely to read through and note any headings and bold print, photos or other items you notice. So you can are able to visualize the chapters you'll be reading through, much like watching the picture of a puzzle before beginning to read it. If you're required to answer questions related to the text, you should read them prior to reading the text. In this way that when you look up the answers as you read you'll know where they're located instead of having to come back to find them. If there's anything you are unsure about, write notes to ensure that your brain can keep a sharp eyes open when the information appears in further reading.

Three Methods of Learning: The Three Main Methods of Learning

Once you have an idea of the broad spectrum of your education It's time to put your feet to the ground and begin gaining new skills and knowledge. There are three primary ways to learn that you can use to maximize your outcomes. The brain processes knowledge in 3 ways: whether through what we look at (visual) or hearing (auditory) as well as the actions we take (kinesthetic). Three learning strategies are grouped under the abbreviation "VAK," which will be further explained in the following paragraphs:

Visual Learners who are visual retain information better through studying, reading, looking at images and charts, as well as watching demos and video clips. Visual learners tend to detect physical signals and are excellent writers and readers. They also are less likely to be distracted by background noises They are typically more attracted by art, rather than music, and would prefer to read on their own rather than listening to audiobooks or hear an individual reading.

Audial: In contrast, auditory learners are the best at absorbing information they listen to and hear. They learn best through listening to audiobooks and CDs, as well as seminars as well as instructions in spoken form. They prefer listening to lectures, rather than read manuals and books, preferring to engage in discussions rather than writing or reading and easily become distracted by the background noise. Auditory learners tend to read loudly instead of in their heads, preferring music to art and are skilled at having lively and engaging conversations.

The Kinesthetic are people who learn by attempting things on their own. They are the kind of learners who enjoy trying things out physically, using their bodies and hands to control and operate aspects of what they're learning. They are able to grasp more of the material when they see how it the process is carried out before them. In everyday life they are accustomed to the routine of taking time while writing or speaking and are physically close or sit near to others when they interact with them. They are generally skilled in sports and other physical activities. They are also physically expressive during conversations, and are always required to be active in some manner.

Every person has certain characteristics of all of the various techniques of learning, however one type of learning is generally prominent in a particular person. If you're not certain of which one is for you, try taking one or two free test online which can help guide you towards your direction. Enter "VAK tests for learning styles" into the search engine and there are a myriad of options to take. Once you've decided that one of these three methods is the most suitable for your needs and your needs, you can apply this knowledge to modify and adjust your strategies. This is particularly important in courses since it is decided by the instructor what their primary method of distributing information will be. If the course is targeted towards a particular method of learning which doesn't work for you, use the information to find resources that best suit your style of learning. In this way, you'll learn faster and comprehend it more clearly. This is the reason for this book. In the coming sections are the ways to modify the information that you are given to help you understand and remember it the most efficiently. Take a look at each and take note of specific aspects of each that you think will suit your needs the most.

Visual Techniques

The most efficient and efficient tools that you can employ to aid your learning process is a learning map often referred to as mind maps. They were created in the late 1990s by Tony Buzzan. Learning maps present a topic visually, and allow you to see the interconnections between different subjects. To create your own personal learning map, turn your notebook horizontally and write down the primary subject you're studying in the middle portion of your page. Next, brainstorm subtopics by with specific phrases or words to group them. For each of these topics create a branch from the central area. You could go even farther and make smaller branches of these subtopics , while remaining relevant to the main topic of each. It is helpful to make them distinct by underlining or highlighting the subject matter in various shades. It is also possible to employ images or symbols to highlight specific words. You can alter the map and customize it to your preferences, and the more you work with these maps, the more proficient you'll get. Mind maps are useful tools to study and revise information.

Other helpful strategies to help visual learners can be as follows:

Place yourself in a place in a place where the instructor can be visible.

Use colors in your writing as you take notes and devise the color-coding system.

Highlight sentences while you read them.

Be sure to pay attention to and study images and charts in your textbooks and handouts.

Draw outline of the data using your own diagrams and charts.

Make use of visual resources like animations and videos.

- Visualize the topics you're studying in your head and create a mental picture.

Audial Techniques

One method of learning that is particularly beneficial for audial learners is the concept of cooperative learning. This is when you join groups of study or a study buddy to discuss ideas, thoughts and advice on the topic. The major benefit to this method of studying is that, if you are unsure it is possible to clarify the topic to one another and then test one another on the subject. In addition the study with others could also bring some fun to the study process.

Other suggestions for learners of audial to use while learning include:

Participate in discussions with your class.

- Ask your instructor questions.

If you are studying you must do it in a quiet area that is free of distractions.

Make small tunes or Mnemonic devices with the materials.

Recite the material loudly and the more effort you invest in it the more effective.

Record your lectures with the tape recorder, or listen them in between the class.

Kinesthetic Techniques

The learners who are kinematic need to be active while learning, taking part physically in the process of learning. The ways to accomplish this are:

Notes - Make notes during class. Then, edit them at home.

Learn the material for the course.

When you're sure you've fully grasped the subject then mark the mark next to the paragraph or section you've read to note it down.

Create flashcards, as well as Post-It notes and then organize them.

When you are studying or reading material, stand up and stroll around.

Don't remain in one place while sitting.

Take breaks regularly to take a break and do something.

Create small movements to help you remember the subject.

Chew gum or eat a snack while you are studying.

Test a variety of aspects in each of the learning categories and gain a sense of which are the most efficient for you. In general, it is recommended to use a variety of strategies that are specific to each category of learning in your process, because our brains use the three aspects. The more diverse areas of our brains we stimulate and stimulate, the more efficient it will be at taking in the information for a longer period of time. It is easy to do this by studying and visualizing information while recording and making index cards for the content. This can be done by combining the strengths of the three methods of learning. It is suggested to select three or four strategies that you have a preference for, and one or two of the two other categories. Although it's the most effective to use your strengths areas of learning, it's crucial to include different techniques from the three categories of the process of learning.

Chapter 4: What is Memory?

What is the essence of memory? It's a difficult to answer, but simply memory is a procedure that involves the storage, acquisition memories, and storing information. It's not all exactly the same, however. There are three kinds of memory. Sensory, short term , and long-term. Before we get into the various types of memory, let's take at the definition of memory.

It is possible to break down the procedure of memory in three stages that are encoding, storage, and retrieval. When data is transferred from a sensory input into the brain, it must to be transformed into a form that the brain is able to comprehend the information, process it and save it. Think of it as changing currency when you travel to a foreign country. The currency you have in the country you're from isn't worth anything until you convert it. The three methods in which this information can be encoded . They include acoustically, visually and semantically. How do you keep the number of a phone? If you can see the number, it means that you're using visual encoding however, if you're reciting the number verbally, then you're using acoustic encode. Research suggests that the main way to encode short-term memory is Acoustic. It means that when a person is practicing for something, for example, a performance or concert the information is stored in short-term memory, and they'll forget the information shortly after the performance or event. The most important method of encoding for long-term memory is semantic, which refers to the process of giving something meaning. Meaning is the fact providing meaning data aids in keeping that item for much longer.

How long will memory last? According to research, the majority of adults can keep 5 to 9 things in short-term memory. We used to believe that memory worked as a slot machine, and the most slots in short term memory was seven. However, if we link parts of information and store them in lots of information in our short-term memory. Contrary to short-term memory, long-term memory is believed to be virtually infinite.

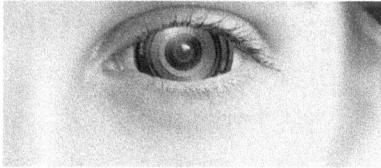

How do you retrieve memory? Everyone has been in the habit of forgetting some thing, be it not bringing your calculator with you to an exam in math or misplacing your keys in your car. The brain can forget often. It happens when the brain is unable to locate information. The way that your brain retrieves information from short-term memory and long-term memory is different. Memory that is short-term is acquired by recollection in a sequence. This means that when someone is asked to keep the sequence of numbers and then has to recall the sixth number of the list, they'll traverse through the entire list in the order in which they heard them before reaching the sixth number. However, long-term memory is stored through associations. It means that if you head upstairs and suddenly forget why you went up there returning to the same room that you first thought about going upstairs could stimulate your memory and help you recall why you decided to move upstairs. Organising your information can aid when getting information out of the brain. Organising is keeping track of time, and sorting them alphabetically or according to size. If someone has provided you with an agenda of things to complete, sorting them into a sequential order like a series of times, makes it easier to remember. Many people believe they are aware of memory. However, the reality of the issue is the fact that memories are mysterious and scientists are only beginning to comprehend the concept. That means that a myriad of myths have been circulating throughout the world and it is important to understand the difference between the truth from the fiction.

The most popular myth. Memory is akin to an audio recorder.

Many people believe the impression that memory functions as a video recorder which is why the eyes are the lenses. This is a commonly held belief for people, since video recorders are the closest thing to memory for a large number of people. In an US survey over 64 percent of participants stated that they believe memory functions as an actual video camera in that it records all the things that we experience and see. It is far from the reality. Memory is extremely volatile as it is easily altered and altered. The researchers Bernstein and Loftus looked at a number of studies that looked into whether researchers could implant false memories in people. The false memories that were examined had to do with food preferences, for instance, enjoying asparagus even though you've never tried it. In one study, participants took part in questionnaires that comprised an assessment of their personality as well as a food history test. The following week, they were returned to the laboratory and told that the results were fed to an instrument that produced an account of their food-related experiences in their childhood. One of the results was that they were either sick after eating hardboiled eggs or felt sick after eating pickles with dill. Following learning of the findings, the participants filled out the same questionnaire on their food habits. The people who were claimed to have suffered from a sickness from pickles made of dill or hard-boiled eggs showed significantly less desire to eat those foods.

Myth number 2: People are able to possess photographic memory. There is a popular belief that certain people possess an inherent talent for taking photos with their minds and can recover the images at a 100% accuracy. However, this isn't the reality. There are remarkable feats of memorization for instance, the memory champ Lu Chao who set the record in the world for reciting pi to the 67.890th digit. However, Lu Chao does not have photographic memory. What allowed Lu Chao to achieve such remarkable feats can be explained by the use of mnemonic devices , and thousands of hours of practice.

Myth number 3: People forget things in the course of time.

People often believe that memories fade as time passes. Research has shown that memories don't degrade as a reel of film. A majority of memories are forgotten instantly following an incident. This is why witness testimony isn't considered to be of high value in the courts of law.

Myth number 4: Confidence suggests a precise memory. The fact that you are confident that the memory you have is true does not necessarily suggest that it is. There are many factors that could improve your confidence in your memory even if the fact that it isn't accurate for instance, repeated questioning. When you are asked the same question repeatedly and giving the same response repeatedly can have an effect that makes the person believe that what you're saying is true. Everybody has different levels confidence in memory recall. Someone can be extremely confident in their memory even though they're not 100% correct all the time. In the same way, one can have a low level of confidence in their memory, even when they are right. Another common myth is that emotions can trigger more precise memories. Experiences that are triggered by an emotional experience are usually remembered with greater clarity, which makes people feel confident that the events took place exactly the way they remembered them. However, in reality they are just as susceptible to distortion as other memories.

Myth number 5: Traumatizing memories are stored and are rediscovered several years after the event. A lot of people believe that traumatizing memories, such as those of abuse in childhood are stored in the brain. They could be recovered through the use of the psychotherapist. Research on children who have been abused show that they don't remember traumatic experiences. When a person's memory is "recovered" it is more likely that the memory was fabricated or dispersed. Memories are not able to be recovered by a hypnotist , for the same reason that memory is not like the video recorder. We do not remember every detail. Evidence has shown that hypnotism may do greater harm than benefit, by giving people confidence on their memories, regardless of whether the memory is reliable or not.

Myth number 6 Amnesiacs do not remember who they really are. The idea that those suffering from amnesia lose their memory for a long time is a myth played out by Hollywood. In reality, amnesiacs aren't able to make new memories. In particular they are unable to convert short-term memories into long-term memories. This is the reason why an amnesiac might be able to inform you about their childhood however they are unable to do so in recollecting the food they had at lunch.

Chapter 5: The Fundamentals Of Accelerated Learning

Accelerated learning, also known as A.L. is currently receiving lots of interest in the present. This is due to the fact that, from a set of ideas and research-based theories, lots of amazing practical applications can be made. There are a lot of research on this topic at the current time. While the reasoning behind AL could differ based on the individual who is discussing it about it, it can be explained with one line. It is the up-to-date combination of theory, techniques and techniques that are focused on increasing the speed and effectiveness of learning. It is true that AL concepts are supported by a wealth of hard data resulted from years of study. A person who has the capacity to learn faster than the average figure is more likely of achieving success in their career. There are many companies and organizations that are in the business and education sectors that have already benefited from the benefits of programs that accelerate learning.

There are a variety of education and learning rules and guidelines that are currently proven to work well for people. The main difference between AL from conventional techniques of education is that it taps into the potential of the brain. Traditional methods leave plenty of space for wasted learning opportunities. AL efficiently utilizes these spaces to increase the speed of learning one can achieve. The approach of multiple intelligence utilization of AL implies that the learning process includes physical activities, music material, tactile, and other things that are related to it. By enhancing the environment the student is located greater outcomes can be obtained.

Based on the accelerated learning principle An optimal learning environment includes:

The root of this can be because positive environment can relax and stimulate the brain of a student. The best way to learn is when they feel an underlying sense of security, peace, and the ability to relax in a certain space or location.

Participation in the learning process is gained best when individuals play an active (active) part in a learning situation. The role of a spectator (passive) role is rewarded by information, but only to a only a small amount.

Allows collaboration between learners A cooperative learning approach which is in use in the present curriculum of schools ensures better quality concepts and knowledge sharing among students.

Learning options are diverse Learning styles are diverse: There are a variety of learning methods that individuals can adopt. The student should be given the option of choosing his methods and methods to learn and master capabilities. Each choice should be based on the style of learning that is preferred by the individual.

The application of abilities and knowledge: This is known as learning in context of usage. Opportunities that are utilized in real-life situations are retained more effectively and for longer.

The focus is on results and allows for new challenges: Students are constantly reminded of their goals, which encourages them to increase their efforts. If an individual is able to clearly define their objectives from the beginning and clear methods can be planned and adhered to.

People who plan to take advantage of the accelerated learning system should adhere to the seven core principles. They are as follows:

Principle #1: The learning process should be a combination of the mind and body.

Principle 2 Principle #2: Learning is about creation , not absorption.

3. Principle 3: Education occurs most effectively when there is collaboration.

Principle #4 The concept of learning is a multi-process process system.

Principle #5: Learning works through the input-process-feedback cycle.

Principle#6 Learning is a direct consequence of positively reinforced emotion.

Principle#7: Learning comes from the power of image processing in our brains.

If we consider the bigger perspective, accelerated learning appears similar to standard learning that has been that is shifted to a higher speed. There are a variety of unconventional methods were a result of the integration to AL into the traditional learning methods we're used to. Examples include the use of classical music within an educational setting, the practice of the practice of meditation prior to reading through lessons as well as the use of mnemonic-based memorization tools.

If you are looking to master the strategies of this system of learning You are on the right track. In the next section, we will cover the very first and fundamental component that makes up the AL system...the human memory. Learn more and begin your journey to becoming an "accelerated learner"!

Chapter 6: Habits and Lifestyle Changes

Development is also a crucial part in the development of your brain. Elon Musk once stated "I believe it's crucial to create an ongoing feedback loop in which you're always reflecting on what you've done and what you can do to make it better. I believe that's the best advice I can give you to constantly consider ways you could do things better, and keep asking yourself questions." Beyond the transfer of knowledge There are other ways to make your brain think faster. There are also abilities that can be applied in any circumstance that aren't taught by transfer learning because of a insufficient time. Here are some tips to keep in your mind to be able to think quickly and more effectively.

Fast thinking on the spot

Being able to think quickly can be difficult, particularly when under pressure. If you follow these steps, you'll be able to deal with any circumstance that requires rapid thinking.

Stay focused on the primary focus. When someone is asking you questions it is important to first be sure you were attentive and understood the question. There are always important words in the questions that you should recognize immediately to give yourself some context and an idea of the type of response expected from you. Examples of these words are the "WH question" words such as "who" "what" or "how," as well as the words that convey the most significance in a sentence. For example If someone asks "why do we think that we are uniquely us?", the words that must first pop into your head are "why," "you," "believe," "we," and "unique." You'll find that these words are crucial in answering the question as they are the words that define the question.

Recollect relevant information. The next thing you must do is make sure that you have access to the correct information within your brain. This is where learning transfer takes place. Through learning transfer, you analyze related information, and then use the information you've determined will be most useful in your current situation.

Once you've accessed the site, utilize this information to respond to the question as appropriate.

Training Fast Thinking Skills

It's great for you to have the ability to work quickly when you have to be able to, but the ability to be able to think at a high speed is a much more valuable capability to possess. If you are able to think quickly, you'll be more adept at sorting out the many different issues and situations you face on a regular basis. However, you will not build this capability in a short time, and the advice mentioned above can only help in a limited way. In addition to knowing and applying the tips from earlier, it's equally crucial to apply these tips to assist you think more clearly.

Imagine "what you would do." It is possible that you are living in a world that presents everything to you in the form of a daily routine. There will come a time when you'll be required to complete an unexpected task. While you're relaxed, work your brain by thinking about scenarios that may require you to think fast. When you think of these scenarios, consider how you'd react to these scenarios. This is particularly important when you're a student. it's not enough to simply believe that the teacher will not make a call just because you're in the back of the room. You never know when your name is going to be called and you must always be prepared by planning ahead.

Learn to speak. Another way to be capable of thinking quickly is the ability to communicate your thoughts in a short amount of time. Try to improve things like the elimination of fillers and tics in your speech, such as "uh" as well as "uhm," use proper grammar while speaking and clearly pronounce your words and ensure that you know your audience well by determining prior to your speech whether your talk can be considered formal, or non-formal.

Be informed. As we've said before it is crucial for you to know a variety of different things. You are able to do this by studying printed material ranging between newspapers and reference materials such as almanacs, encyclopedias, and encyclopedias. Thanks to the internet, it's easy to get access to the latest information. Utilize technology to stay in touch of the latest developments and trends in the world, particularly for situations that you are likely to encounter in your daily life.

Do mind-training exercises. There are many activities for your mind that can aid in the development to think quickly. These are some of the best ones you can test to see if they work for you:

Reading comprehension games. One of the most popular is to read the chapter of a book or article as quickly as you can, and then you should give yourself at minimum 30 seconds to write down the information you've read.

Recite names or words for each one of the letters as quickly as you are able to.

Games that make use of timers can be helpful too.

The internet is full of apps as well as online quizzes specifically designed to enhance the function of your brain.

Play improvisation games.

Prioritize tasks. Utilizing a calendar, note the things you're planning to accomplish in the coming weeks or days on your calendar so that you don't need to use your brain to recall them, permitting you to commit your brain to activities which can improve your brain's performance.

Utilizing these suggestions will aid in improving your cognitive performance. Regular practice is likely to improve your cognitive abilities over the long term.

Chapter 7: Master any skill quickly and easily

You and your coworker have both been web-designers for an advertising firm. You both earned the same bachelor's degree . However, you were in within the upper 5% of your class, while he barely got the test. You both want the same opportunity He took home the bacon.

What could be the cause?

The world is changing, and what attention-grabbing efforts individuals used to pay to formal education is now being replaced by new skills which give businesses and organizations an edge in the workplace. No one else is to blame.

As the world becomes increasingly fast-paced, mastering skills in one area might not suffice to keep pace - let alone grow your career. We are entering an age of multiple intelligence so the better you understand more about it, the better chance you will be successful.

Learning new abilities isn't the easiest thing to accomplish. If you do it the traditional way it could take years to master the new skill. The research suggests that the process of learning a new skill will take around 10.000 hours. That's many hours. If you take the math you will find that it would take about 416 days of no sleep or breaks.

Who is able to spend that much time?

The 10,000-hour Myth

The ability to practice a particular ability for 10,000 hours takes a amount of commitment and discipline. If this is a fact that cannot be changed what do you say to an individual who becomes incredibly proficient at learning a new language skating, or painting in just a week? I'm sure you've experienced something similar at one point in your lifetime, but the reality is that it's not the norm and it doesn't necessarily make you the status of a genius.

The reality is that there's more to the 10,000-hour rule that what the average sources of information explain. The incredibly long hours were discovered by researchers who looked at the best performers with complex and advanced abilities such as track and field, as well as Chess. It's normal for athletes and cognitive abilities to require more time to train. Particularly, in the event that you're planning to become an all-star.

If you're not looking to be an A-level and the aim of your practice is to become better, not be the best, the process of learning a new skill might not be as difficult as you believe it could be. It's likely to not require 10,000 hours of your time.

The results of Kaufman's study show that it's possible to master something new within a reasonable amount of time. 20 hours, to be precise. How do you change from an impressive 10,000 hours of work to 20 hours?

However, the author and trainer Tim Ferriss said that it will take anywhere from 6 to 12 months before one could learn a new skill to an professional level, or what he views as the top five percent of the population. Language, he emphasized it can be acquired and utilized in just eight to 12 weeks!

Both of them suggest that learning new abilities is easy but one will need the proper methods and motivation in order to start.

What hinders people from learning an New skill?

Sometimes, we encounter extreme difficulties to begin the process of learning the new skill. We typically blame it on external as well as internal factors like the lack of the time, capacity, capabilities, and the like. In reality, we do have the capacity to be able to learn something new - we simply hesitate to take the plunge.

Here are a few reasons that prevent us from mastering a new skill:

Fear of Failure

Don't begin something because you're afraid of failure. You may be not comfortable in dealing with negative situations, so not participating in the sport in the first place is the most secure option to protect your self-esteem and pride.

Imagine that you have taking the test for language proficiency. Instead of trying to improve your understanding of a particular language you put off the work, and then relax with the thought that it's OK to fail since you've didn't even try to pass it anyway.

Feelings of frustration

The process of learning a new skill takes effort and patience. You will usually go through many trials and errors before mastering a particular technique. This, naturally, is necessary, but isn't something to be considered a weakness by people who are hesitant.

Imagine that you're learning the basic job of baking shortbread cookies. The first attempt came out burned, your second resulted in a salty mess, and the third one looked like a painting by Picasso. After a few attempts, you're still getting nowhere. After a while the energy that has been accumulated from failure makes you want to get angry and stop everything. It is your goal to overcome this desire and stand up to your most formidable adversary - yourself.

Too Many Distractions

There are a lot of ways we can go about learning the latest ability. But the "many things" aren't always productive. We don't get off to learning with a strong start because of other things which take our focus. The famous saying says, "You cannot serve two masters simultaneously." That's why you can't study a new language while watching your favourite Netflix show at the same time or learn the use of Photoshop while playing"Assassin's Clead" online.

They are fun, but as enjoyable as they might be, could consume years of your time without your realizing. They generally serve a useful purpose, for example, they can be an effective outlet for stress. But, doing it excessively can affect your life negatively. In this case, stifle the desire to discover something new and provide you with more reasons to delay your learning.

The illusion of not having enough Time

This fact is in line with the previous one in that we are programmed to think that we are able to learn something new if we were able to do it. I'll tell you something You're never going to be able to learn enough unless you alter that mental model.

The phrases "I'll learn the fundamentals of Japanese when I have an hour of free moment" or "I am unable to learn how cook because I have so much time off from work" are falsehoods you create to avoid (1) failing, (2) frustration, or create more time to (3) other activities that distract you.

The negative forces constantly try to drag us down and prevent us from being more efficient. The challenge is in how to overcome these forces to constantly improve our abilities as individuals and professionals. The sooner you discover this motivation, the quicker you'll be able apply the methods and techniques needed to learn quicker.

How to Maintain and Gain Confidence Essential to Learn the new skill

When it comes to learning skills the process of overcoming the negative forces requires the assistance of a positive force. Therefore, the most effective way to get the motivation to acquire an ability is to combat any doubts, fears, and excuses by reaffirming your beliefs with positive reinforcement. Here are the major advantages we require to keep us motivated:

Simple and Practical

Before starting any project it is crucial to assess the level of difficulty and examine the resources we have in order to ensure that all the information necessary to learn the new skill is feasible and easily accessible. It is also suggested to look at the skills that we already possess and consider how they could be used to learn the new skills. An list of the things you are able to accomplish and the things you'd love master can assist you in making an effective starting point.

Complex skills will take more time and effort. They are also more likely to cause disappointment after several unsuccessful attempts. If you're only starting your journey to acquire skills It's ideal to begin by focusing on something that is easy. Since, more often than not, basic skills have a higher chance of success. If you are successful in your first session of training for your skill will certainly increase your confidence in mastering a specific ability.

Early Results

Each new skill that you master each new skill, you will receive a time estimate of the amount of time it would take you to learn it. If the difficulty increases, so does the amount of time it takes to work on it. It is important to realize that not all abilities are of greater value. Sometimes, simple abilities prove beneficial in the real world. It's just a matter of knowing which ones produce the greatest results in the least amount and resources.

Cooking, for example is a difficult art that can be reduced into a simpler version. In the book, The Four-Hour Chef, written by Tim Ferriss, he let us in on a small secret that will help me and you, as well as everyone other person in the world in general, cook like a top chef. In addition to being able to relate to cooking, it provides the essentials you need to master the most specialized skills that are known to mankind.

A sense of accomplishment

After having completed each session with success and recognizing that your new ability is producing tangible outcomes (being capable of conversing with the Chinese native after having practiced

Mandarin over 10 weeks for instance) will give you an overwhelming sense of satisfaction and a huge confidence boost.

Being aware of your ability to learn and being able to prove your progress helps you believe in yourself more. This increased confidence is a major factor in encouraging you to pursue the training process and improve your abilities - completely removing the majority of your fears and doubts about trying something new.

Accelerating Learning Skills

It's Sunday. In your home Sunday is laundry day. There are six people in the same house and you're the one on call. There's a lot of diverse clothing, each of which is an individual color, and you're aware that some shades don't work with other colors, particularly those with clean whites. There's so much to choose from that it's difficult to begin or complete. After several sighs, and with whatever energy you've got left, you began sorting your laundry according to colour and kind.

A couple of hours later the laundry area was clean and tidy. You wondered how you were able to complete everything in that short amount of time. But , hey, everything is fine and everything is good.

The above example is a metaphorical illustration of a technique known as deconstructing. It's the act to break down certain ability into smaller, nitty-gritty sub-skills. In the laundry day scenario, it's when the large pile of clothes was sorted out into groups that are similar. Every skill comes with two or more sub-skills that can be identified using the process of "clustering" which is the process of placing things together that are similar. In this case the task was completed faster once the clothes were separated. This is the same when learning new skills.

If we break down a skill that seems daunting into attainable sub-skills we can speed up the process of learning. Imagine this in this manner:

Before you begin learning how to bake, you'll first have to learn how to mix, whisk, sift and prepare. You won't be able to rise from your bed in the morning and decide that you'd like to bake muffins. In the beginning, you must know how to prepare the muffin batter before discussing baking them. So, we can say that learning the fundamentals first is the most efficient way to mastering an entirely new technique.

Another important technique is selection.

The ability to keep your attention on track for long periods of time is difficult enough on its own, but especially if you're expected to be exhausted for a long period of time. Are you imagining having to memorize the words you'll need to know upon waking and before bed each day? The mere thought of it can cause you to cringe.

We are fortunate to have other strategies.

Did you know that by altering the method you use, you can alter the speed of output? You can help make learning new skills quicker by altering the way you approach your learning. Like studying a language it will take you years to master tens of millions of vocabulary . And those are only words. Making them palatable, changing the Tenses, and creating sentences of your own are all difficult areas to tackle as well.

However, how do we reduce the number of people to a mere 22,000?

You may be thinking it is impossible for a single language to consist of only two thousand words. That's true. However, no one has ever claimed that you have to master every single term in the English dictionary to engage in meaningful conversations using the language. This leads to the procedure known as selection.

Instead of having to memorize random words every day, why not learning a few common words and phrases that you'll likely require to use. It's surprising to discover that it only takes four words multiplied by a number of tenses to have a lengthy and meaningful conversation in another language. It's all you have to do is fill your vocabulary with terms you know are necessary for daily use and communication becomes an easy fill-in-the-blanks.

Making Skills Last

After you've worked out the most difficult aspect which is mastering a new skill quickly and efficiently, you are faced facing a second issue: how to ensure they last. Everyone doesn't want to put their time and effort to wasted effort, especially after going through many difficulties to accomplish something.

Skills are a bit like relationships. They become dull when you don't keep in contact. The world is constantly changing and the skills we have are constantly evolving in order to keep up with the demands of today. If we don't improve our skills regularly the time will come when our new skills will be obsolete.To keep the flame burning and the fire burning, keep in mind the two P's:

Practice

Perhaps the most well-known one in the book, but nevertheless an essential. Continuous practice is vital to keep the quality and precision of a ability. It prevents you from getting out of the game and helps you keep up-to-date with current trends. However, it requires the discipline of self-discipline and dedication, which makes it difficult for many to keep up their commitments when years have passed.

Personal Merit/Demerits

In our daily lives, we acquire and master a range of capabilities. This number is multiplied when we take it upon ourselves to master more. This makes maintaining much more difficult. It is a commitment to practice, however when you're dealing with so many items, maintaining everything isn't just a hassle the task becomes impossible.

Therefore, the best way to preserve them is to enhance their value. Like how we hang the objects we love that have emotional or financial value, our skills are more durable in situations where they are a source of merit or aid in avoiding an omission. It's a lot more effective to learn when there's something in danger, isn't it?

For a refresher we can recall the lessons we learned from this chapter:

The ability to learn new skills can give you a advantages in and out of in the workplace.

Learning skills can be accelerated with the proper methods and techniques.

The main obstacles to developing skills are anxiety about failing, frustration or disorientation, as well as the impression that you don't have enough time.

We can ward off the negative effects of these forces by reversing them with positive experiences in learning.

By breaking down the skill into its sub-skills, and then learning the skill using a bottoms-up strategy accelerates the process of acquiring skills. (Deconstructing)

When it comes to skill-training there is no need to be able to comprehend all the things. Just focus on the things that matter. (Selection)

Continuous practice and setting a particular value on the ability can assist you in maintaining and improving it over an extended period of time.

Chapter 8: The Goals You Set Your Goals

To reap the most benefits from the book, it'd be beneficial to not take each chapter as a unique advice for self-control, but it is also important to view the whole thing as a whole. Based on this, I think it's time to go over what we've learned so far in chapters 1 to 4 is appropriate.

In the first chapter we looked at what self-discipline means and where it originates and why, in order to become a more disciplined person in our lives is a crucial quality of life. In chapter 2 we examined the importance of creating your own personal schedule and adhering to it is of essential importance in maintaining self-control to ensure that you don't flit around randomly toward whatever you'd like to. Then, in chapter 3 we discussed how to avoid excess and maintaining the balance of your life will allow you to keep taking the straight and straight path and avoid slipping back into your previous habits. In chapter 4 we talked about the massive differences between motivation and discipline and how being able to discern the distinction can ensure that your performance does not diminish over time.

After all the knowledge so far, you'll have a solid foundation from the ability to begin practicing self-control. I'd also suggest that the final chapter can be considered not mandatory, but I do hope you're able to push through until the conclusion (as an aspiring self-disciplined individual and you shouldn't have any doubts about it) since it's my goal that this chapter will provide you with crucial information on how you can apply the knowledge you've gained from the chapters 1-4 to your own goals.

In the book I've included numerous mentions of the different desires, hopes and aspirations of every man as well as a children on the planet. This chapter will not be an exception. In this chapter, we will concentrate on gaining self-awareness so that you can examine yourself and find out what your goals are and the best way to begin to achieve your goals with the highest achievement.

Childhood might have given us various ideas of what we'd like to do in our lives, (becoming an astronaut, cowboy, doctor, among a handful of other professions) the years between adulthood and adolescence tend to provide the majority of people with an entirely different perception. Of course, this isn't at all the fault of anyone. The world operates in a different way than people believe in the absence of any knowledge of the world. As children, many of us have grown up having things handed to us and when we reach adulthood it is a shock to discover that society does not take into account what we would like It seems to attempt to stop us from having that desire.

This isn't single person's fault; instead it's all of us's. Every single person is trying to achieve some thing, or accomplish something. It makes sense there will come a time two people who share the same desire will attempt to achieve the same thing, even though there's only enough for one of them, whether it's a job, or a relationship partner or something else. The result is usually it is that the one who has the lowest amount of commitment and self-control is likely to fail, and the other person will be able to achieve the success they both desired.

It's not to say that anyone can't achieve the goals mentioned above even if they would (although the idea of a cowboy may not be the exact thing one would have expected since there's more than just herding) However, generally, they're confronted with the same issue we talked about earlier in this chapter motivation. They see a dazzling image of the job they'd like to have or girl they've been obsessing on however, they are only seeing the final result. Like if they've time-traveled to the enthralling career or with the beautiful woman, and then they imagine them achieving these goals without weighing in all the commitment and determination that are the prerequisite to be successful at all.

The spark in the beginning could be viewed as essential, as without those young people with starry eyes who had the courage to dream that our society could fall apart. We'd be faced with an acute shortage of lawyers, doctors, and cowboys. However, the only ones who are being successful in these positions are those who have discipline, as it's not just about having the motivation to accomplish something, but being committed to pursuing this desire.

In this regard, I'd like you to set aside a few minutes to consider your personal goals. If it's one you set as a child or one you're currently pursuing simply take a minute to think about the idea. Consider the reasons you may have been unable to achieve it. I'll wait.

Did you do it? Because I did. What I discovered is probably what you'll find also: that the outcome was one you wanted however the route to reach it wasn't fleshed out enough to allow you to take the steps needed to get through the path.

From now on I'll give you three specific steps that will assist you in overcoming this mistake, so that you actually begin to get a better idea of what you have to accomplish.

1. It is important to narrow that goal down

The biggest issue that people have to face when they attempt to achieve an objective is that the purpose is too broad. A person might say, "I want to be a doctor" or "I would like to learn how to play guitar" but doesn't consider that these are just general phrases. Do you want to become a surgeon? A pediatrician? An anesthesiologist? Would he like to learn how to play the electric guitar? Classical guitar? Do you want him to be able solo or simply chords?

All of these are the things one should think about before pursuing any objective. If you don't ask them, you'll be at a crossroads with no clear idea of the direction you'd like to follow.

2. Break it up

Okay, now that you've narrowed down the things you're looking to accomplish and you've decided to create your strategy. This, in essence this, is what sets your self apart from a self-controlled person: you've got your dream and a strategy to turn it into a reality. It may feel great having finally decided on what you'd like to pursue however, don't pat yourself on your back overly. Most importantly do not even attempt to imagine the end of the road as it's a good opportunity to be discouraged by the sheer amount of work ahead.

Many people may disagree with me on this point because they believe that the "eyes at the goal" approach is the most effective. It is possible to clearly see in your mind's eyes the goal you're working towards, and as a disciplined, self-motivated human being, it's fine since you'll reach it at some point, you think?

Well, not quite. If you do take something from this book I'd like to think you'll recognize the flaw in this way of thinking. Sure, you should be aware of the final outcome of all the hard work will be (otherwise how will you be aware of what you're trying to accomplish?) However, it's vital to avoid long-term thinking . Try to break down your ultimate goal into smaller objectives so that you don't become exhausted. In the fourth chapter You must think of the achievement of your target as a marathon that requires long hours and effort - not a sprint that you only reach after exerting yourself for a short time.

6:1 rule

When you've decided on a goal , whatever it may be - and after you've narrowed it down, it's beneficial to look at that it's not just one huge target, but rather a set of smaller goals. The individual checkpoints let you to take your time and make sure you're making greatest progress you can.

Depending on the objective you're trying to achieve is, it may contain a dozen, or thousands of small goals. However, for reasons for time and space, I believe the 6:1 rule will perform well enough. Let's return to the instance of learning how on the guitar. Your 6:1 could look like the following page:

Chapter 9: Utilize Multiple Learning Processes

One of the worst characteristics of any educational system is to depend on a single method of learning to teach all students about a specific topic. The system does not consider that people learn in different methods. While some students might be capable of reading notes written by the instructor on the chalkboard or Textbooks and understand the material in the same way but others will struggle to keep the knowledge acquired through this method. They'll require different methods of learning to make the information be absorbed into their minds. This is why using different learning methods could make all the difference to the world. Utilizing multiple methods of transmitting information, you are able to utilize different parts of your brain in order to reach the desired end result. Instead of learning with your eyes, you can also use your hands, ears and other senses of touch to learn, comprehend and master the new material you have learned.

There are three primary styles of learning that are utilized by all in one way or an alternative. The first is visual. It focuses on reading or watching an activity being performed. Students who excel using this method of learning are more likely to get better grades at school, since the visual method is often employed when teaching in general. They will be proficient in studying by reading notes and using flash cards to reinforce information. They also excel in projects for research as research usually requires a lot of reading. Many of them even possess photogenic memories, which means they are able to recall what they read, even after only reading it only once or twice. Although it may appear to be the work of a genius but the reality is that everybody can recall information, provided the information is properly delivered at the beginning.

The other method of learning is called auditory. This is dependent on listening to the material being taught. A lot of times, students in a class will be picked by the teacher due to the fact that they're not looking at the instructor during the lecture. The majority of the time, students will be able to answer the question quickly and clearly, proving that they are paying at the lecturer's words. was speaking about. It isn't some technique that students use to trick the teacher, but rather is a sign that these students are studying the subject through auditory learning. To pay more focus on the words of the teacher auditory students often glance at their backs, which allows their eyes to be focused on what they're listening to instead of what they're actually experiencing. Through focusing their eyes to focus on nothing important, they can train their minds to forget about their eyes, and thus pay all focus on their ears. This is the reason they will get the solution right away when their teacher asks them to do so. They only absorb the information they hear. So even although they may not appear at all attentive, the reality is the instructor is paying all-time attention.

The third type of learning is called tactile learning. This is often called 'hands in learning'. Students who require tactile learning require doing things for themselves to comprehend how the thing operates. Hearing and reading instructions only help them as they need the act of doing it as an instructional tool. The people who learn best by doing things with their hands are typically people who excel in fields that require hands-on work in nature, like woodworking, mechanics and sewing, cooking, as well as art. Anything that can be executed and handled with hands is something the tactile learner can comprehend quicker and more deeply than those who depend on reading or lectures. In addition, anyone who thrives on reading or listening will usually struggle in any class that is more focused on the tactile aspect of learning.

Understanding the three types of learning is crucial to accelerate learning due to two primary reasons. When you've figured out the method that is most suitable for you, then you can use this method first and increase the effectiveness of your efforts , without needing to increase the amount you commit. So, if you're able to prefer to learn by listening to instruction as opposed to reading it, then you'll be looking for audio tools for learning like audiobooks, CDs Internet video and the similar. If you prefer tactile learning as the method you prefer, you'll want to find an area in which you can try out the subject you are studying since hands-on practice will make a huge difference in aiding you in mastering the subject matter you are studying.

Another reason this information is important is because it allows you to employ a variety of methods of learning to master the subject faster and efficiently. When you mix the three styles of learning, you'll be able to engage different areas in your brain engaging more brain cells throughout the learning process. When you listen, read and physically participate in the subject, you'll be engaging all aspects of your brain, which means that the knowledge becomes part of your entire brain. This will allow you to remember facts more quickly and accurately since you are able to trust the things you learned, heard, and experienced directly. This approach to learning that is multi-system is the one utilized by those looking to master subjects quickly and efficiently regardless of the difficulty of the subject.

Chapter 10: Listening and Skills for Listening to Enhance Your Memory

We've already talked about the ways that good listening skills improve your concentration and in turn improve your memory. In short, when you pay attention to something, you efficiently and effectively encode the auditory data, and when you are constantly focused on it, it transforms into long-term memory can be easily retrieved from your memory banks whenever you need to.

To make sure you are listening to the things you need to There are a few strategies you can employ.

Focus on the source of auditory input, and then focus on it.

If you're constantly fidgeting during a podcast whether it's a friend telling you their story or a speaker giving an address at a seminar that you're going to, or a podcast that teaches you how to accomplish your goals, you'll not be able to pay attention to it in a focused manner.

Be aware that information received through various senses that relate to the same subject often creates a blended well which helps to consolidate the information more effectively. If, however, you are exposed to different stimuli that relate to various themes, you'll confuse everything and cause confusion within your brain. In the blink of an eye you'll be exhausted and not able to concentrate on anything.

If you are listening to someone or something don't fumble or do anything else look at the source of your audio like an MP3 player your TV or speaker directly, and keep your eyes on it, regardless of whether it's an unliving thing. Directly facing the object or person means that you won't be gazing around instead, you will concentrate on it with a keen eye. This allows you to build and keep your concentration on the source of your auditory information and hold onto every word that comes to your ears to process the information in a timely manner and encode the information precisely.

Reduce background noise

If it's the sound of the vacuum cleaner humming in the background, or the blender whirling away at the fullest If you hear background noises while you're trying to listen to something, you won't focus on it as much.

To ensure you're able to take note of the information you're looking to process, try to reduce the background noise, and attempt to eliminate it completely. This is feasible when you are in control of the surrounding environment, like your home or office. But, if you have a space shared with someone else you could ask them to reduce unwanted noise for a short period or use noise cancellation technology or work even when you're on your own.

Ask questions

There are times when you're unable to recall something due to the fact that you don't comprehend it clearly even if you're hearing it perfectly. A good listening ability goes beyond than simply being attentive to something. They also require that you comprehend the subject thoroughly. When you fully comprehend something it is possible to will be able to effectively encode the information and then transfer it to your brain's long-term storage capabilities. A great way to achieve this goal is by asking questions while you are listening.

For example you're in conversation with your board partner or a potential business investor acquaintance, friend or any other person about something that is important to you and that you wish to recall details about you can ask the person a series of important and profound questions regarding the subject. Be attentive to what they say and ask them thoughtful questions taking into consideration your conversation's context and the goals you and the other person want to reach.

If you're watching a lecture, podcast or video that you want to study and save to your memory note any significant thoughts that pop up in your mind. You can then look up the answers in the future. When you're certain about an idea that you have learned, it will become deeply embedded in your head and be part of your memory for the long term.

Picture

As explained earlier in the text, when we visualize things in your head and focus on it, you are more focused on the image. Utilize this method to get lost into the experience and to open your eyes and your mind to pay attention. While you listen to something, don't just listen to it through your ears, but also think about it with your eyes. Whatever you're listening do your best to create a vivid visual image that you can visualize in your mind.

Take note of words key words, crucial keywords, points and the elements, then use these to draw sketches of your thoughts and focus on the sketch. If you can visualize something while listening, you trigger your brain to concentrate more on the subject, get immersed in the experience and also encode information more effectively. Effective encoders lead to solid consolidation and the successful retrieval of information.

Keep a curious, non-judgmental and open mind

When we watch something or someone, like videos it is more than just listen to our ears. We also listen with preconceived notions stored in our minds.

We judge what we hear based on our own desires for superficiality as well as societal norms and stereotypes, and our preconceived ideas. This affects our ability to think objectively and impartial state of mind. Despite the fact that we might think that we are making rational, independent decisions however, often we are paying attention to biased information.

Making informed, sound choices that work for you over the long run and make you feel content and content inside can only be achieved through a calm open, rational, accepting and unprejudiced state of mind. In order to achieve this it is essential to listen with an open heart.

If you're listening at something you don't think about what you will conclude and you don't put labels on everything. If you notice any preconceived notions pop up and is trying to dictate, keep in mind the importance of listening clearly and unprejudiced, then refocus your focus towards the discussion.

Note important details when you need to examine the information with a clear mind. This allows you to see things as they really are, and delve deep into things with clarity and understand all the facts to the fullest extent. Once you have a better understanding of things it is easier to retain them in a clear way.

Try LACE

LACE (Listening and Communication Enhancement) is a program in software specifically designed to enhance your listening abilities. It consists of five distinct listening skills that are designed to enhance your listening, communication and cognitive capabilities. This includes:

Processing quick speech

Identifying a specific sound from a loud ambient

The need to fill in missing words in conversations

Improved auditory memory

Concentrating on one voice among a variety of voices.

Find out the details about LACE on this page. Once you have a solid understanding about how it functions utilize the program consistently to achieve the desired results.

Spaced repetition

You are more likely to recall the news you received in the past than what that was heard in the past few months. In the field of psychology, we call this the "forgetting curve. This happens since our quick-term memory doesn't last for a long time. With a limit of just some seconds, or even several minutes, our working memory disappear when we do not strengthen the ideas we have. Spaced repetition is an effective method to strengthen your memory and prevents the process from happening.

If you are listening to something, be attentive and, within a couple of seconds you should try to recall the information you read or heard. Then, you can use flashcards or repeat the ideas by speaking them out loud in order to check your recall. You can repeat the process multiple times, spacing them by 2 to 5 minutes intervals between.

Slowly, expand the time between repetitions, and repeat it following a gap of 10 minutes. You can do this for 20-30 minutes when you are dealing with complex and important information, and then for 10 minutes using less complex information. You'll quickly transfer it to your memory over time.

Try to remember mnemonics

Mnemonics are awe-inspiring memory improvement tools which aid in the consolidation of information and retention. They employ elaborative encoding imagery and retrieval cues assist you in acquiring facts quickly, then commit it to memory and later retrieve it as needed.

There are many kinds of mnemonicsto choose from, some of which we will be discussing in later chapters, for this we will concentrate on the musical mnemonics and acronyms when they are closely related to speaking and listening.

Acronyms are abbreviations that are short for generally longer phrases, strings of words, a complete sentence, or even the word or phrase is longer to help you remember an idea or series of words or concepts. For instance, 'Everygood Boy is Fine' an incredibly popular acronym to remember the treble clef EGBDF. In the same way to it is the case with Great Lakes: Huron, Ontario, Michigan, Erie and

Superior have become the standard acronym "HOMES.'

When you need to recall a difficult part of information, make an entertaining acronym and sing it out loud, over and over and in a clear way to imprint it into your mind and put it into your long-term memory. It is also possible to create an entertaining, fun tune around the subject you are trying to remember and sing it loudly. While doing this you can also use the other strategies as well to better remember it. For instance, you can visualize the words you're using and practice spaced repetition and then listen to it without judgement to increase your understanding of concepts.

Names, things, etc. in a conversation

If you're talking to someone and you would like to keep track of their name, or some other information or particulars about him/her then mention that information multiple times during your conversation. If you'd like to recall that Janet who you have just attended a conference with works as a speech therapy therapist, and has a clinic in Boston in Massachusetts, mention her name several times during the conversation. You can also ask questions about her work.

If you'd want to learn how to speak in public, follow the guidelines that you have just learned from a talk made by a friend Engage the other person in a discussion regarding it, and then repeat the rules several times.

Repetition helps information get absorbed into your memory making it easier to remember and access it whenever you need to.

Keep a record of yourself

To make a better grasp of the information you're retaining and to help you remember it, you should record yourself while you are doing it. Make a tape recording or take a recording of yourself using your phone's recording device to track every fact or figure you talk about. It is then necessary to listen to your recording several times as you practice your words or information you've recorded aloud.

When you revisit your account over and over again it gets buried deeper in your memory and is able to turn into your memories for the long run.

Chapter 11: Understanding Yourself As A Learner

Deceiving ourselves into thinking that we don't need to re-learn is the worst type of deceit.

--Plato

We all know the genres of books we love reading. Some people love thrillers but do not enjoy science fiction. A different group prefers biographies or books on history. The same is true for our food preferences. It is possible to like Indian and Chinese food vegetarian or nonvegetarian rice and potatoes and the list goes on.

How do you learn? In order to be a proficient learner, you need to understand the type of person you are. If you do not take the time to research it is possible that you are believing that you're not capable of accomplishing something when you really can. What is it that makes your approach to learning distinct? What can you do to enhance the areas of your life that aren't fully developed?

Three of them are key elements that define the way you learn:

1. Whichever you decide to learn

2. It is easy for you to process the facts

3. How do you deal with the information you've already absorbed

We've talked about this first factor earlier. Now, you must reflect about the effect the two other determinants can have in your daily life.

We all thrive in different contexts, absorb information in different ways and process it in different ways. The truth is neither John or John is superior to either of them; both possess appropriate skills for work and at home.

We will discuss the way in which information is absorbed by the brain in the beginning

How Information is Transformed

The five senses are crucial in aiding you to process information. The five senses integrated by your primitive brain also known as the brainstem. They are hearing, taste, and touch as well as some vision.

The sense of smell, however, is carried directly to the amygdala as well as the olfactory nerves within the limbic system or mammals' brain. So our senses of smell are among the fastest way to register. It is possible that your survival relies in our capability to distinguish the smell of meat "wrong" and the smell of our competition!

Most of the time, one sense dominates over the other

Utilizing Your Senses

The three most common ways to get information are through your eyes or your ears, or via your body. You see things or listen to them and become involved in engaging with them, often with the touch. What is the most effective way to absorb information? Utilizing your eyes, your ears, or even your body?

The majority of the time, do you need to sit straight in meetings , and then try to direct your gaze at the eye of the speaker?

• Would you like to be reading rather than be read to oft grabbing information from other people?

Have you found it simple to recall an individual's name over and over again?

* Would you prefer to use maps or follow instructions in a text?

* Are your clothes typically coordinated?

Are you quick to switch to charts and illustrate problems with drawings?

If the answer to most on these is yes, are relying on your eyes the to the greatest extent.

Are you able to repeat phrases that have been said by a presenter, or smile in agreement when you are spoken to?

Do you often gaze into space and dream while you talk to yourself within your head?

Do you like listening to radio or music?

Do you ever lose your name?

* Would you prefer to be guided by a verbal message?

Do you enjoy telling jokes and enjoy a lively debate while solving a challenge?

Do you like using your smartphone?

If the answer to all the questions above is yes then you're extremely dependent on your ears.

* Do you often sit in a slump during meetings and feel frustrated because you're not able to move around and get up?

* Do you like playing with your diary, pen or even rubber when you're talking?

Do you like outdoors activities?

* Do you find it easier to recall events than the names of people or their faces?

* Do you create facial expressions using your body?

* Would you prefer to act and take action to fix things yourself, rather than wasting time and arguing about it?

* Do you enjoy conducting business and doing an activity simultaneously?

Do you have a positive answer to all on these concerns? If yes, then you're dependent on your body for the most part.

Many people have a better time absorbing information by using these various methods. Certain people, specifically those who've made an effort to create different styles may prefer one or two of these. Most of the time, in a group, around 30% of people are naturally comfortable with their eyes, another 30 percent with their ears; and the remaining thirty percent of their bodies. Each method is not better than any other and they're all different.

Most workplaces require distribution of information occurs through written or spoken instructions. In the majority of training rooms, also in meetings, individuals do not typically feel compelled to get up and walk about, but that's the way that a large portion of people would like to do.

Handling Information

The way in which we deal with the information that we absorb by our senses is contingent on our character. The person we are an important factor in determining how we perceive information. To make it simpler the concept, two people can see the same image and observe different aspects.

This becomes even more obvious when there are words involved. When someone tells that you "That would be a great idea," you could be hearing one of the two choices below:

It's a good idea. Perfect! The conclusion is that I am pleased that he agrees with me. I'll proceed to purchase the flights.

This is a good idea. It's also the case with every other suggestion we're considering. We'll need to find out more information before we can make a choice to fly or take an train or take a rental car and chauffeur the entire group.

Carl Jung was the first to offer a comprehensive explanation of this idea[2Carl Jung was the first to provide a detailed explanation of this concept[2. Jung classified people as sensors, thinkers people who feel, and intuitives. Jung's ideas are the foundation for many of the tests that are used to determine the personality of a person. A test that is frequently utilized tests test is called The Myer-Briggs assessment of personality. Its purpose is to determine the person's personal preferences.

There are 16 basic personality types and are based on four primary types: intuitive thinkers sensitive feelers and sensing feeling. The four types react in predictable ways and in a variety of ways as they accumulate information and perform their actions in the real world. For instance, the sensory thinkers prefer to rely on undisputed facts, while intuitors prefer to base their decisions on their general perceptions. One of the benefits for the test Myer-Briggs is it's unbiased and suitable for both the home and workplace.

Figuring Out Your Learning Style

Peter Honey and Alan Mumford each British psychologists have developed an assessment test that is widely used across a variety of organisations. It is built on three components which determine the individual's style of learning, the way data is processed. It offers four different learning styles that include reflector, theorist activist, and pragmatist.

Without further research Which one of these is the best description of your personality in learning?

Honey as well as Mumford's explanations give an accessible way of putting the knowledge you've acquired into practice. Although they don't explain the fundamentals of a reputable style but they do provide a practical and realistic perspective on the personality of your learner.

Being an activist you're the type of person who can quickly take control and begin. You are a fan of instant experiences and you're enthusiastic by new things. Most of the time, you react first and then think. You love engaging in activities that you enjoy, and when you face the problem, you begin formulating different strategies to solve the issue. You're probably a social person.

Your catchy slogan is "I'll try everything once."

Reflectors typically avoid encounters. It is likely that you would prefer to be in the back of the room during meetings. Before you make a decision, you prefer to take in a wide range of facts. You are a person who likes to take a step still and look at the direction of the situation before presenting your thoughts. You're very cautious when you are in nature.

The catchy phrase is "I'll need to think about it."

As an theorist, you tend to see things in a series in logical order until you transform it into an order. You are a fan of rules, systems and models. You enjoy being calm and rational. You are a deeply pondering person and are not willing to be with an opinion because it doesn't align with your personal beliefs.

The key word is "But what does it have to do with into."

As a pragmatic person, you are always keen to test out new ideas. You're extremely experimental. You'd like to complete things fast and without taking time. If you are able to hear something intriguing you'd like to be able to experience it right away

Your catchy slogan is "There must be an alternative."

Chapter 12: Uneffective Methods and Learning Myths - How Not to Train Your Brain

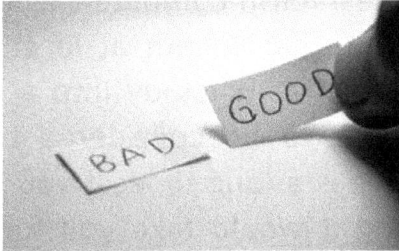

"We should not be hindered by myths from the past when we focus on the needs of today."

Harold S. Geneen

Although there are many methods to train your brain, practice and study carefully, and dedicate yourself to mastering new techniques but there are numerous strategies and myths that are not effective, or worse, they can be detrimental. It is essential to stay on in the right direction and adhere to your study habits to avoid falling into these harmful ways of thinking or get sucked in by the myths.

The 10,000-Hour Rule

In the past the 10,000-hour rule has been utilized to establish competence. The rule says that you has to put at least 10,000 hours of practice or study into a specific skill in order to be considered to be a master. This is a long time. If you studied all day long it would take you for nearly 417 consecutive days before you could be known as an expert. In the context of humans having to sleep, eat and work, as well as raise children and manage other personal matters What could it take to finish 600,000 minutes of studying time?

Nowadays, this legend has been debunked. Individuals learn at different rates and imposing a specific amount of hours spent studying on any skill is now obsolete. There are some certifications and professional certificates require a specific amount of time for the task in order to be considered proficient but the old rule is generally no longer in use.

In recent times experts have suggested that it's best to seek out external opinions to gauge the level of your knowledge. You can find a tutor, mentor or coach to assist you in assessing your proficiency in your chosen field. Feedback can provide you with direction about areas where you can improve and what you should call 'learned material' and help you decide on the next stage that you learn.

Making a Choice

Another myth that's been around for many years is the idea one is either left- or right-brained and that this is dependent on dominant hand usage. This has led to the notion that right-handed people with left hands are more artistic and creative as well as left-handed people are more analytic. This theory is completely false.

In reality, everyone uses both brains equally, therefore there's no need to classify yourself according to an idea of using the one brain more efficiently. Lefties, you are free to get some math skills up to date! Right now, you can go to the store and purchase some art equipment!

The Myth of the 10%

Another common myth about the way we use our minds is the one that claims we utilize approximately 10% of the capacity for our brains. The evidence now suggests that human beings throughout one day, consume 100 % of their brains but not at the same time. This implies, unfortunately, that there's no superpowers that can be found in a brain that is completely locked, as certain common myths of pop culture suggest. It's better to seek out cosmic clouds and radioactive spiders to be superheroes. Research suggests that the way we research has a more profound influence on the brain's development than the things we do. Keep in mind that the brain is an developing organ and is constantly changing and firing.

Disclaimer: This was a comic book prank. Be careful not to expose yourself dangerous substances or conditions while trying to attain superpowers!

The construction of Pyramids Pyramid

Like the many theories about the way in which The Great Pyramids came to be constructed at Giza However, nobody is completely certain where they came from. Learning Pyramid theory arose. According to the Learning Pyramid theory states that the person's memory is based on proportions of 10 percent of the things they've read 20 percent of things they've heard 30 percent of things they've witnessed, 50 percent of what they've heard and seen 70 percent of items they've written or spoken about in addition to 90 percent things they've done or taught other people.

In reality, this isn't the case and you shouldn't be basing your learning habits on the pyramids of learning. Experts in education say this is a myth and that the percentages can't be verified with neuroscience or biology.

Intelligence is a fixed Point

Intelligence, as well as how we view intelligence is a key aspect in the way we learn. Contrary to what we initially believed intelligence isn't a fact by birth. Yes, people can get smarter. Intelligence is measured in IQ (intelligence quantity) since the very beginning of tests at the beginning of the 20th century. The tests are designed to gauge not only the things you've learned but the ability to discover.

There's been a shift towards a move away from the raw IQ scores in recent times because they do not tell the full picture of an individual's abilities Recent studies have shown that intelligence can be enhanced through studying. For many years, students were classified based on their perceived intelligence and the majority of lower IQ students were considered to be weak and didn't have the ability to grow. It is now clear that this was to be false.

Another issue is that it uses the idea of a high IQ to encourage students. This often leads to a backlash; when students are celebrated for being smart and smart', they aren't convinced that they are required to study to be able to comprehend. This usually leads to poor habits of study and poor results when those students enroll in institutions of higher education. They may be smarter than others however those who are hardworking are the ones that will get their goals met and will be given opportunities.

The middle path seems to be to concentrate on achievable goals with a small size that are all geared towards the end goal and avoid letting others create false impressions about your intelligence. Don't let yourself be deceived about your own capabilities also! Be sure to give yourself praise and others for the time you to learn and not just for the IQ.

Following Your Gut

Always stick with the first choice! Do you remember the middle school multiple test of choice? In reality, you shouldn't be doing that. While it's been widely believed that the mind would spontaneously produce the necessary details on the first attempt but that's not the case at all. It requires critical thinking to review your answers to an test or quiz. There is no evidence from science to show that your initial answer is higher probability of being right than a solution that you make up after having second thoughts. Your first gut reaction answer isn't necessarily incorrect However, if it's possible look over your answers and find out if they're accurate.

While the suggestions above pertain specifically to formal learning environments however, it is applicable to adult or in independent learning settings as well. Critical thinking is an essential element of being a successful learner. Being in a position to evaluate your own performance is a good means of measuring your own performance against the standards. If you have an instructor or mentor They may also conduct some sort of test to gauge the progress you've made, so you'll need to keep your skills for taking tests up to date.

One Thing at A Time?

The traditional belief was that learning strategies required a single and focused for them to be efficient. It's not the case however, and you learn more when we mix things up in the routine. Today, in our schools teachers are using multi-media methods to learn and as an adult student you can use these ideas for yourself too.

While you're learning do not bind yourself to an uninvolved routine that you're bored and lose interest. It is important to keep a constant flow of your knowledge make sure you do it by combining studying, visual aids and even film. You can try changing your study location - go outdoors on a sunny day, or even set up various backdrops on the computer. Sometimes, a change in pace is required to help your brain reset. Keep in mind that one of the main goals is keeping your brain awake enough to retain its the ability to change.

Nobody wants to feel like they've slowed down.

Imitation is the Most Beautiful Form of Flattery

While this may be the case but what isn't certain is that mimicking or imitating experts can assist you in learning more quickly. The experts who are knowledgeable most about the subjects you'd like to know are excellent sources However, they required many years of study and hard work to get the point they are today. Just copying them won't provide you with any real knowledge.

Instead, look at their work and make use of it as a study resource. Many advanced students, like scientists or professors at colleges have published articles in journals or written books. Experts are in each field who publish regularly in trade publications. Find out from where they're getting their material from and find out what their journey to becoming experts was, then pick the articles that will assist you in your own study. It is a fact that you, as a newbie is not able to learn the same way as experts however this is matters to your level of expertise. All of us must be learning at the right pace and this pace is determined by our personal experiences.

How to Get Rid of the Myths and Have Fun with Time

In this article, we'll discuss the good, bad and the wrong of study methods and methods, we've covered the word TIME numerous times. It is essential to reserve time to study and practice, however life can be a source of adding obligations. With only a few hours to study, how can this time be efficiently managed? In the next section we'll into consideration how you can focus your efforts and make the most of your the amount of time you spend studying to meet your objectives.

Chapter 13: Active Learning

Learning is often in the form of passive. Students sit in a class for hours and watch a professor or teacher present an instruction. The only stimulation they receive is through their ears as they absorb into consideration the words the lecturer is saying. Sometimes, they may also experience visual stimulation but they do not actively participate in the process.

The passive learning method isn't as efficient than active learning. When students play an active role, they can learn and retain information quickly.

What exactly is Active Learning?

Active learning gives students the opportunity to become involved in the subject they are studying. Alongside listening to the instructor, they are able to engage with the subject through writing, reading or asking questions, and then discussing what they've learned, as well as on any new information.

It could be useful to consider the method by which we learn to use words to give an illustration. Teachers can sit in front of the room and explain a word to you by writing it down on the board and then defining the meaning. But the students most likely to keep the word and incorporate it into an integral part of their language are the ones who talk about it in conversations and think about it.

The benefits of active learning

Let's discuss the advantages that active learning can bring to your life. These are:

Active learning assists in moving information from short-term into long-term memory, because you are required to utilize what you've learned in a variety of ways.

Through the use of multiple types of learning (verbal and visual, auditory and so on.) active learning improves the likelihood that you'll learn because everyone has various learning abilities.

Active learning will help you improve your learning skills by sharing the methods and techniques that are the most likely to allow you to excel in your classroom.

Active learning fosters problem-solving abilities and increases critical thinking skills by allowing students to be engaged in the material they are learning.

Students who engage in actively learning methods are much more excited about learning than those who are learning in a sedentary environment.

As you can observe, there are many important benefits of active learning.

How to Include Active Learning as a An Essential Part of Your Life

Teachers might utilize active learning to help students learn However, even if teachers do not, you may apply it to your own time for studying. Another area in which it can be beneficial to study with a friend or group. You can discuss the concepts, exchange details and thoughts and make use of your time with each other to better understand the lessons you've learned.

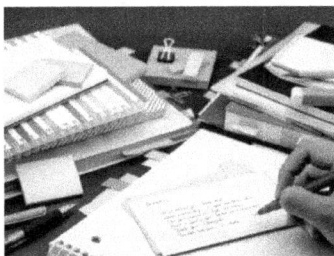

Even if you're studying by yourself You can still integrate active learning into the activities you study. For example, you might:

Make flashcardsthat include writing. Then, read them aloud to incorporate listening and speaking into the mix.

Create pictures or view videos that relate to the subject you're studying.

Find real-world examples of what you've learned and analyze them in a critical manner.

Make time to think about what you've learned, and place it in context with other subjects you are familiar with.

These strategies will help you remember the information you have learned and can make learning something you are looking forward to.

Of course it's not the only technique for accelerated learning you could employ. In the next section I'll discuss methods you might be able to benefit from as you continue your study.

Chapter 14: Your Memory

Have you been to the supermarket and don't remember half of the things that you were looking for because it was too busy in your mind to write an inventory list? This happens even to best and the worst.

There are many advantages to keeping track of everything you have to remember and many drawbacks to not remembering everything! Let's see if can come up with methods to get rid of the drawbacks and appreciate the benefits of having a great memory.

There are some easy fixes you can make to improve your memory. The first thing I'd like to discuss is sleeping. If you're not sleeping enough, and you're always exhausted your brain is not working as efficiently as it should be. The best method to increase not just your memory but also other aspects such as your ability to comprehend new concepts is to ensure that you're receiving at least nine hours of rest every all night (for adult adults). If you're in your teens or early 20s, you should strive for up to 9-12 hours of sleep each night.

Everyone is aware that exercising is an incredible thing can do to your body's fitness. But did you know it can also boost your memory significantly? Running, jogging or cycling are all things that can be done for 20-30 minutes, a couple of times per week to help you retain information better. There's a portion of the brain referred to as the hippocampus that is extremely vital to your memory. While exercising, the blood flowing to your brain and the hippocampus. This increases the size and the memory bank.

It's another way that you can take care of. It's starting to seem like a diet book Isn't it?

It's true, though! Making sure you are providing the proper food and energy that your brain needs is something you cannot fail in. If you're eating nutritiously to stay healthy and trim your brain requires good fuel as well! A variety of foods, including fish blueberries, broccoli as well as dark chocolate, have been proven to improve memory and enhance the function of your brain.

Meditation can also assist you to improve your memory. Studies have proven that focus and concentration improves your memory capabilities, all of which meditation can help with. When you practice meditation it is a matter of taking your mind off and focusing on something else, not the events in your daily life. The purpose is to calm your body and mind, and take your mind off things.

Drinking water is an aid to many those with memory issues. It might seem strange since it is water. It is certainly beneficial for digestion and your body however, how does it beneficial to your brain? Your brain is comprised of 73% water. This means that being well-hydrated is vital.

Before we go on to some of the techniques for speedy learning which can aid you in improving your memory, here's one other thing you should look up. I would suggest taking a an examination of any medication you're taking. A lot of people don't realize that certain medications may have negative effects on memory and may cause you to forget information that you've been able to remember for a lifetime.

How can you increase your memory with accelerated learning? The best answer you and I along with the Internet can provide are brain-based games!

Engaging in games that enhance brain function , and playing brain teasers is similar to performing a vigorous exercise on your mind. There are numerous games you can play to stimulate and stretch your brain while also enhancing your memory. Some of the games can be played include crosswords and jigsaws Chess, chess, as well as Sudoku puzzles. It is essential to not play these kinds of puzzles often but. When you are doing this, you'll stimulate other areas of your brain but not your memory bank.

Chapter 15: Speed Reading Techniques

The ability to speed through text isn't an ability you can acquire in a matter of hours. You must commit to practicing sessions, just like any new ability.

Words in Groups

When you read your book, your eyes is on each word. To speed up this process it is necessary to learn to focus your eyes the words in groups. Begin with three words.

Exercise 1:

Read a book and try to jump around the text, paying attention to 3 words at each. In your head, you should pick some words when you're doing so. At first there is no need to consider which words you pick. It's just a matter of practicing the method of jumping across lines of text with three words.

At first glance, it may appear as if you've read an incoherent, jumbled chaos. At this point you don't have to care. It's the same way that running athletes would train during a warm-up. Through this method you'll become more adept at speed-reading. As time passes, you'll discover that your brain and eyes are focused on what they consider to be the most important words. Other words are omitted as we can see in our sentence examples in

If you're reading words in groups on each page. Let's go towards a method of leading you on the page. This is called meta guiding which is also known as the pointer technique or even hand pausing. All of them are trying to achieve the same result to guide you on the page.

Exercise 2:

You'll require some sort of card and a ruler. When you were young and beginning to learn how the art of reading, you might have used your fingers as a guide through every word while you read it aloud. Don't just use your fingers now, as you will need to stop the lines that follow to learn this method. By blocking out what's moving farther down on the page your eyes will be able to focus on what you're studying.

Continue reading phrases in groups but put your card on the line you're reading. You'll need to move your card quickly in order to reach every line. It might seem awkward at first, but eventually, you are getting your eyes trained to focus on the line being read.

When the ruler or the card can slow you down you can change the marker you use to your finger or pen that has a lid to make sure you don't draw the text.

Once you have mastered these two methods Once you master these two techniques, you will:

* Skipping words

* Reading groupings of words instead of individual words

* Reading scans much faster

Try these methods with less difficult reading materials, like magazines or nonfiction books.

Highlighting

You're now ready to take notes on what you're studying.

Exercise 3:

There will come a moment that you don't require a marker. Once you reach the point where you are able to begin to note down the words your eyes are able to pick up. In the beginning, it could slow your reading back down however, it will allow you towards the next step. Notes don't have to be understood in this moment since you're still learning the process.

Take a look at your work. Are your words logical? If they do, you've understood the text using this revolutionary way of reading. If not, you should continue practicing.

This is a way to read the text before reading it, and you could do this throughout the entire chapter. The notes you record will help you decide whether you'd like to revisit the book to get more details. If you decide to do so it, you will be able to re-read the important parts and skip those parts which are not of any use for you.

As you will see, it's not as much about reading every word in a rapid pace. It's about navigating the text quickly in order to locate some key words. You can then determine where the text is where you have to pay attention when you read it again. It's not similar to the harmful habit of reading the same phrase, paragraph or word repeatedly. This is about figuring out the location in a whole book, and then laying out the crucial details.

There is also the possibility that when you read the headings it allows you to skim through a book quickly.

These reading tips add up to assist you in learning the process of speed reading.

Benchmarking your new skill

To be able to see your progress as you work to improve your speed reading it is necessary to create a basic form of benchmarking. This will assist you in analyzing your own performance.

It doesn't have to be an arduous procedure. It could be as easy as synchronizing your body with the same workout every day. If you notice that your progress slows or stops and you are not able to continue, try the next exercise.

If this occurs then you are assured that you're improving your speed reading abilities.

Five Tips to Improve the discipline of Learning new skill sets

Daily exercise

This is crucial for you to ensure that you don't lose any improvements you've achieved. Every brain exercise you do alters the chemical makeup that your body produces. The neural pathways inside your brain will expand and grow, meaning that your brain is in the process of getting better. Once you've cleared the initial hurdle of kicking off the development of new brain cells, you'll never go back. It's not an easy task however it'll be worth the effort.

Everyday routines

The new habits you are developing should begin with your new set of skills. They should be an integral part of your daily life naturally. Research is showing that when you keep your brain healthy it's a method to lower the chance of developing dementia.

Challenge your skill levels

Always strive to enhance your skills and limits. Do not let any skill be inactive. If you can improve the skills of speed reading you not only enhance your speed reading abilities but also improve your general knowledge. This will make you be more secure and happy with your life. It's going to be a lot of work, but you will reap the rewards of a upwardly mobile career or just a feeling of incredible satisfaction with yourself.

Redeem Rewards

Your hard work will pay off as the areas that you've made your lifestyle better. Speed reading enhances your reading abilities and allows you to take advantage for a progressive lifestyle. Now you can anticipate:

* An increase in your job.

Health improvements by understanding the importance of living a healthy life.

* You'll be able to experience increased feelings of happiness and satisfaction. All negative feelings that you have experienced previously will vanish out of your life. You might even want to help others solve their issues as you break out from your cocoon, and utilize your new skills to travel the world.

Make sure to take your care of yourself.

In the modern world it is crucial to take good care of yourself. Don't forget the importance of yourself. It's not selfish to take care of your body and your mind. It is common sense. You can accomplish more good in the world when you have a well-balanced mind than prior to opening your mind to self-improvement.

Chapter 16: The Procrastination Effect, Procrastination, And Learning

According to studies, approximately 88% of students at colleges from America United States are guilty of procrastination. The study also estimates that around 2 out of 10 students across the world suffer from procrastination chronically.

Procrastination is the primary cause of being unable to effectively manage your time and focus it on important activities like learning. It's a major obstacle that prevents you from getting results, and can hinder you from reaching your goals, such as learning the new skills.

If you truly would like to learn about difficult subjects, quit putting off studying today.

But I'm sure this is a lot easier to say than done. Psychology classifies procrastination as a mental disorder that is considered an unavoidable habit. Therefore, it requires the effort to fight it completely and beat it.

The first step to combat procrastination is knowing the reasons we put off completing our tasks.

Common Causes of Procrastination Common Causes of

Our brains are drawn by immediate gratification

It's likely that you've got you're Twitter, Instagram, or Facebook profiles open in a separate tab on your computer or iPad that you're reading this book. It's so tempting to visit it once the future, isn't it? Research has shown that instant gratification exerts more influence in influencing our actions than delayed satisfaction.

We are looking for perfection

Perfectionists are the best procrastinators. Many people are prone to procrastinate even in their studies because they anticipate too much and aren't happy about not meeting their high expectations. For instance, you may decide to put off doing maths due to not being at the right level of motivation. People who are perfectionists believe that it's more beneficial to complete an assignment with a half-hearted effort, so they can maintain their conviction that they can have accomplished the task with a lot of effort rather than putting in all their energy and produce a subpar outcome.

We don't like the subject.

It is possible to put off taking the accounting test as you might not enjoy the subject. It is difficult to read accounting books only to discover that you don't know the basics of accounting. When you put off studying you are hoping that you don't have to go through the entire book and instead, you can scan your notes before taking the test.

Or maybe we're just busy.

Time management is essential to understanding anything. If we don't manage our time and we are juggling many obligations at work, school and at home it is easy to neglect to make time to gain new things or develop new abilities.

Strategies to Avoid Procrastination

Below are some suggestions that you can implement to aid you in fighting procrastination.

1. Be aware of your behavior

The way you conduct yourself can assist you in determining the precise instances and times where you are procrastinating and aid you in overcoming this destructive behaviour. The only thing you need to do is make a note every time you put something off.

Take note of the things that prevent you from doing your homework: a constant thoughts in your head that keeps coming up, a constant recall of things you don't like physical pain, a lack of concentration, or a lack of motivation.

2. Learn in a productive setting

To avoid putting off the most important task like learning a new language, it is essential to set up an environment where you are able to maximize your learning. For instance, it is difficult to focus on your studies while in your living room watching TV and other distractions. Make sure you take the time to prepare your study space before you begin to learn otherwise, it could lead to procrastination in itself. Once you've started learning you must be free of electronic distractions. Simply open the books and files you require from your computer. If you aren't using an Internet connectivity, switch off Wi-Fi and turn your phone into airplane mode.

3. Debunk Your Myths

Imagine the learning project that you're currently in the process of delaying. On a piece of paper take note of all the reasons for the delays. On the left side, record your reasons for the delay.

Myth No. 1

-- "I Learn More Under Pressure"

Debunk

There are different ways to make yourself feel pressured apart from being patient until one day away from the test. For instance, you could establish a time limit (2 hours to complete chapters one and two of the novel) or you could pretend that your work should be handed in after two hours. If you follow this method for between two and three months, you'll be working on a draft of your manuscript , and you've experienced the actual process of writing novels.

Myth No. 2 -

"I Must First Perform This or That Before I Begin Working"

Debunk -

If you are faced with a new learning task it is easy to find things you need to complete before you begin working cleaning your space first, check your email and wait for someone to arrive home and so on. However, the reality is that you're making excuses as a way of procrastination.

Myth No.

3 "I must work for two hours in a quiet environment in order to make the most of my education"

Debunk -

A continuous work schedule of two hours is not enough in your head. You can instead master the subject in one-hour chunks or shorter. This way, you're breaking down your project into smaller chunks, so it is easier to manage. Focusing on a particular part of your project for an hour makes the job easier to handle, and you'll feel more motivated to not put it off. You may require a longer hours of work to achieve your goals. Therefore, as with other strategies in the book, when this one is not successful for you, put it aside and consider other methods.

4. Find an anti-procrastination partner

Find someone you are comfortable with and ask him or you to be your anti-procrastination buddy. It could be your college friend, your coworker working at the office, or your mom (default anti-procrastination buddy in reality).

Inform your partner of your learning objective and timeline . Ask for their help in determining whether this plan of learning is feasible. Your partner should alert you when he/she is aware that you are doing nothing instead of studying. Make sure you have an open discussion regarding the issue. This approach can assist you to return to your mindset and help you keep your goals in mind.

5. Be realistic with your time frame

One way to combat procrastination is to develop an understanding of time. We are often unrealistic about how we view time. "This material for studying only takes 4 hours to read," you say. "Hence there's no reason to wait in the evening before the test."

You could be not realizing that our lives are packed with activities aren't considered. For example, at night prior to your final test, say you visit the coffee shop to have a drink with your buddies at 4 after 4 pm. The time you spend there is an hour. Then you go shopping (45 minutes) Then you took a buses (30 30 minutes). Then you cooked your dinner (45 minutes) followed by washing all the food items (20 20 minutes). When you return to your bedroom to begin reading, it's 8 at night. However, when you open the laptop you discovered that you received five emails, so you went through them. It's 8:15 at night. If the subject really takes an entire four hours to master You'll be awake until early in the morning at 12:30 and that's not include the minutes you spend looking at Facebook and Twitter. Facebook and Twitter news feeds.

You've discovered, the subject is more difficult than what you initially thought the exam, and you've completed the exam in five hours. You were up until 11:30 in the morning however, you realize that there's less chance of getting top marks on the test.

6. Utilize a Weekly Calendar that is not scheduled.

If you have a deadline to meet You should attempt to change your schedule. This method will enable you to make a realistic plan of when you'll be working. It's a weekly schedule that will assist you to list all the different ways that your time is currently allocated. Include not only activities that are related to your education objectives, but also other tasks like your meal, personal chores and errands cooking, and getting together with your buddies. This will give you with a complete picture of the time you're spending on other activities besides studying.

Unscheduling will also show blank spaces. These are the exact times to plan your work. Utilizing these as a guide you will be able to accurately estimate the amount of time you will spend on your learning every day during the course of the week.

This method is also a good method to get you started on your path towards a bigger learning endeavor like writing a book or earning a master's degree. You might think you'll need a long time to achieve these goals If you actually define the time you'll need each day, you'll be able to see that you need to start soonerrather than later.

Additionally, this method will help you understand how you're doing with your time. You may be shocked by how much time you're scrolling through your social media feeds and you might want to make some adjustments. It is important to include enjoyable and entertaining activities into your agenda, so that you don't end up having fun while you work (another way of avoiding work).

You could also make use of an in-between calendar, to track your progress toward the goals. Each time you write your novel, for example you should note it by marking it on the calendar. One of the best methods to stop procrastination is to provide yourself with a reward every time you complete a task that is related to your objective even if it is just a tiny portion of the overall. The ability to record the progress you've made on paper will assist in strengthening your productivity mindset and you'll be motivated to complete more work.

7. Set Timeline

Perhaps one of the primary reasons you don't finish your work is that you don't like the work you're doing. Most likely, you excel with numbers, and writing is not your forte area. Therefore, you'd rather solve endless math problems instead of writing an essay. In this situation it is advisable to establish limits for the time you'd like to devote to it prior to doing any other task. Although the reminder "Should write that essay over the weekend" isn't likely to motivate you to compose, "Work on the term essay for an hour" can change your outlook.

The Pomodoro Technique, discussed in Chapter 4, can help you take on tasks in smaller chunks, which can help you to finish large projects.

8. Forgive Youself

According to research, allowing yourself for the mistakes that you commit (such like procrastination) will help you stop the bad habit. This is a method of acknowledging that you are in control over the habit and you can alter it the way you do it if you choose. Do not be too harsh with yourself, and allow it to go.

9. Shut Off Social Media

Social media networks like Facebook, Twitter, Instagram and Pinterest are amazing technology that allows us to connect at any time to anyone any time, from any location. However, a constant scrolling through newsfeeds could harm your education.

The research suggests that the time spent on Facebook can affect the grades of students. Facebook also affects your focusas you check for notifications, statuses and updates frequently can significantly hinder your capacity to absorb information.

The best way to prevent this is to unplug your social networks. There is no need to quit your profile and put aside the photos of your cat that you adore. Simply avoiding Facebook while you're engaged in exercises for learning could assist a lot. It is possible to complete a task for an hour and not check your Facebook profile. Gradually increase your endurance by increasing the amount of time you block out, for example three or four hours. Once you've gotten rid of social media, you will take more time to work or have fun offline and relax.

Exercise

To gain a clear view of how much time you're losing by procrastinating, you must make the effort to track the way you spend your time.

In the coming days, be sure to carry a notebook that will record the amount of hours you've spent doing every task. Keep track of even the smallest things, like making meals and bathing or even going to work.

The idea is to get a clear picture of your current situation in order to determine the amount of time you're spending every day and pinpoint the areas where you're spending your time.

This activity can be a good way to get you thinking about put procrastination into context and inspire you to act.

Chapter 17: Techniques to Enhance the Quality of Your Memories, Their Consolidation and Retention

To increase your memory and keep information quickly, you need to develop the acquisition of memory, consolidating and retention skills. These are the three steps of creating a memory and remembering it.

The first step is to go through each one of these phases to help you gain a better comprehension of each. We will we will then go over ways to increase your capacity to grasp new information and remember these.

Memory Acquisition

To retain any information you must master the information first. Learning information (what is known as"information acquisition) is the very first step of the process of forming memories. When you attempt to understand something, your brain first transforms the information into neural pathways that are temporary and this information is then an element that is stored in short-term memory because the memory is just beginning to form. Most of the data stored in your short-term memory fades in time, but the memories that are effectively encoded within your brain, the ones that you pay close focus on and you remember frequently, stay active for a long time.

In order for any memory that is short-term to change into a more long-term memory it has to be encoded the brain. In most cases, you will have difficulty recalling things because you didn't encode the information to your brain. Therefore, in order to increase your memory improving your memory, working on it is just as important as keeping it.

Memory Consolidation

When you have gathered a particular item of information, you must consolidate the memory to be able to remember it in the event of need. Consolidating information is a second phase that takes place. For any information to be remembered it is

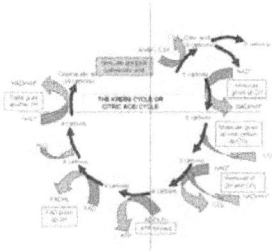

necessary for the brain to convert the data into long-term memories.

You are able to recall items that are within your memory of the long term because the brain is constantly filtering data stored in the short-term memory. This is crucial to ensure your brain doesn't get overwhelmed with unneeded irrelevant information. You is able to concentrate on the important things.

In relation to memory consolidation, which is the process of turning every bit of information in to long-lasting memories, it is necessary to strengthen the neuronal pathways associated with to the information. Memory consolidation can be described as the process by that the strengthening process of particular neuronal pathway occurs.

Numerous factors play an important role in the process of memory consolidation. Of these, the two most important are the connection of the new information to memories that are stored in your long-term memory and the emotional effect of the new information. If a specific item of information is tied to an existing memory and profoundly affects your emotions it is likely that you will be able to recall it forever because the neuronal pathways that it connects to get stronger within your brain. When a specific memory develops and is consolidated, you can access it from your long-term memory.

Storage and Memory Recovery

The third step is retrieval of the procedure and is the exact step you must complete to save any information. The retrieval of various items of information requires different amounts of time. In general, the better acquainted you have with one particular item of information, and the more you can remember it, the faster you'll be able to retrieve the information.

For example, if you have a habit of memorizing the order of elements from the periodic table multiple times per day, it'll only take a few seconds to pull that information out of your memory. You could need perhaps 20 or more minutes to recall the same pattern. People who have still trying to remember the information, or who have already been through it several times might take several hours to remember the pattern.

Additionally, since the neuronal activity patterns of memories connected to one another are similar and you often recall things that are similar while trying to recall specific information. For instance, if you are trying to remember the name of the first film by Will Smith and you keep recollecting the title of his latest film because the neuronal pathways for both elements of information cross.

To enhance your memory and improve your ability to retain information, you have to increase your capacity to absorb new information, store it, and later retain it. The ability to acquire memory is essential to store information effectively within your brain. The consolidation of this information improves the neuronal pathways that are connected to the information. The ability to recall information faster will ensure that you remember an important item in the shortest amount of time.

Let's see what you can do to accomplish everything:

Strategies to Increase Your Capacity to Learn and keep them

The strategies below will improve your ability to collect information, organize, and keep information.

Mnemonic Devices

These well-known and frequently utilized tools enhance your memory by allowing to consolidate the most difficult of data. Memory improvement techniques that use mnemonics help you remember information quickly by helping you link the information with pictures and phrases, words and sentences.

Below are some of the most powerful mnemonic devices you could utilize to boost the neuronal function of any important information that you have learned, so you can remember the information whenever you need it.

Form Acronyms

Acronyms are shortcuts that you can employ to help you remember difficult string of information. This method lets you select the initials of the phrase or word you wish to learn and arrange them to create a catchy name or phrase you can learn. Students learn how to recall all the name of the five Great Lakes: Huron, Ontario, Michigan, Erie and Superior with an acronym called HOMES.

Another Mnemonic tool closely associated with acronyms is the acrostic. Acrostic, a punchy word that you can use to remember the short form of a word, bit of information, or a series of facts. For

171

instance, the majority of people remember the notes on the bass staff 'ACEG' , with the aid of the acrostic "all cattle consume grass.'

When you face a large or difficult chunk of information to remember put it together according to the order you'd like to be able to remember it in. After that, remove your initials for each word to create an impressive acrostic and then repeat it.

Then, read it out loud along with the significance at least fifty times, and then note it down on many post-its. Place them in different locations around your home or at work so that you can go through it fast every when you encounter it. This will help you to consolidate the information that you have fed in your quick-term memory which will help transform this memory into a permanent one. If you repeat the phrase often, it will become easier to remember it at the right time.

Utilize Imagery

Visual imagery is a powerful technique for mnemonics you can utilize to memorize the names of people, places as well as any other thing that appears difficult to grasp. In order to use it, you need to link the information you would like to master with different images that appeal to you.

If, for instance, you're constantly thinking that your boss "Shauna loves her coffee with two sugar cubes and one teaspoon of milk imagine your boss floating in a pool black coffee, with two sugar cubes surrounding her and a teaspoon milk in her mouth. Although this may sound funny and might seem absurd but just think about this scenario for a moment and you'll not forget this info again. Every time you need to remember something crucial and complex use this method and you'll never have difficulties recalling the information.

Model Mnemonic

Model mnemonic is a fantastic tool that you can utilize to remember difficult procedures in biology, chemistry math, botany Physics, mathematics, and many other disciplines. You can also utilize it to keep track of the details about your company or other tasks you handle for the company you work within or for your own business.

In order to use a model mnemonic it is necessary to depict the information you intend to master by using chart, pyramid circular sequence model 5-box sequence, pie charts or graph, or any other manner that gives you to remember the data. For example, if you transform your Krebs Cycle into a circular sequence model, and then divide it into quarters and focus to master one quarter at a go and then move onto the next, you'll quickly remember and remember the entire process.

Utilize these Mnemonic tools to embed complex pieces of information in your brain, allowing you to recall it easily. Another way to accomplish similar is to use the mental snapshot technique.

Mental Snapshot Strategy

This is an excellent method to learn the names and faces of people. You can remember their names anytime you need to without having to repeat a string of "hmms" or "I'm sorry that I did not remember your name" each time you meet people you've met before and who you would like to develop a relationship with. People are annoyed when they are unable to identify them or remember their name, especially when you've met them at least once before. The lack of memory creates a negative impression, and the person on the other side is more likely to avoid you next time they come in.

To make sure this doesn't occur to you and that you don't lose chances to create solid relationships, you can use the mental snapshot method to recall and remember names faces, names and other vital information about your contacts. To test it, try these things:

When you meet someone who you would like to see again to build rapport them, and they will become your friend, take a photo of their face. Select the unique facial characteristics and snap it. We refer to this as a "face snap. For example If you meet someone with a large nose, pay attention to the large nose and snap an image of his face.

Create a name snap of this person. Names can be classified in two groups: names with meanings that trigger images and which do not invoke an image in particular. For example, Brown, Bishop, Long, White, Charlie as well as Dick can be names which invoke visual images, and also have an underlying meaning. I have a friend who is known as "MasonWhite. To recall his name when we got together I thought of a mason working on an all-white building. This is how I effortlessly remembered his name, even after having forgotten it twice. For someone to make their name snap begin by determining the class to which their name is a part of. If her name is associated with an image, you can use it to create the name snap. If not, make use of the syllables of her name to create an image that is believable. For instance, to remember the name "Sandy Clarks Imagine Clark Kent (Superman) relaxing on a beach.

In the end, you can join the name snap with the face snap with images which combines both photos. For instance, a friend of mine is named Will Crawford with large, brown eyes. My face photo of him is his beautiful brown eyes, and his name snap shows Will Smith dancing with Cindy Crawford. When I put these photos together, I can imagine Will Smith and Cindy Crawford applauding my colleague's beautiful brown eyes.

Utilize this enjoyable, fun method to remember names and faces of people, and quickly build up good contacts.

Make Something Unique and Fun

Alongside these things, you should also incorporate the activity of your choice that is fun and creative to your daily routine, and then regularly perform it. Why is this so important? A study carried out by researchers from the Michigan State University proved that those who participate in creative activities like crafting and art have improved mental ability as well as a higher likelihood to be living a happier life, compared to people who do not take part in creative activities.

The creative activities provide you with an opportunity to break away from routine, make you explore the possibilities and engage in something fun. This improves your cognitive abilities and allows you to think more effectively and to absorb and store information faster, and then retrieve the information quickly.

To get the most benefit from this strategy try something new every day. You can enroll in classes or an arts program and learn how the art of playing an instrument, create something with wood, or create DIY projects at your home. If you aren't sure if you're able to devote the time or money to take a class, you can take a look at coloring. It's much simpler than drawing since all you need to fill with the spaces already in place, but it is still a challenge in choosing colors and coloring methods. Coloring adult coloring books are readily accessible and there are several affordable and unique coloring books from Mindful Coloring Books. It is not necessary to be a genius in any way simply enjoy it and for the purpose of stimulating your mind to think creatively. After you have tried any kind of creative endeavor a few times, you'll start enjoying it and will be more likely to continue doing it for a long time.

These strategies are focused on improving your mental abilities, so that memory retention increases. There are many times that you'll need to master new abilities. The next chapter will discuss quick and efficient methods to master new skills and improve them.

Conclusion

Next, follow the strategy that we've laid out and apply it to your learning objectives, no matter what they may be, and achieve mastery over your subject or ability that you choose with precision focus, speed, and concentration. The ideas outlined in this book work equally well with almost all subjects, from cooking to sports , academics and music.

If you've been working through this book while you read through it and then began preparing and taking your first self-directed, accelerated study course as you learned about how it works, great for you! Every time you try rapid learning to master a new skill it is actually helping you gain capabilities that will help you in your accelerated learning process however, in all cases I suggest you keep this book in your pocket to refer to it as a useful reference to further research.

In the last section, acceleration learning can be an tool that you can utilize to move through your life and over the course of your life to learn. To put it in the words I suggested back in the beginning of the chapter: perhaps you've been transformed - a convert to accelerated learning as a method that could, in positive ways, impact your life in the years to come as you develop and grow.